Once
Upon
A
Revelation:
About Islam

BY

Will Clark

Once
Upon
A
Revelation:
About Islam

Published By
Motivation Basics
P.O. Box 6327
Diamondhead, MS 39525

Will01@aol.com

For more information visit the author at:
AuthorsDen.com

QUOTE

"A nation can survive its fools, and even the ambitious. But it cannot survive treason from within. An enemy at the gates is less formidable, for he is known and carries his banner openly. But the traitor moves amongst those within the gate freely, his sly whispers rustling through all the alleys, heard in the very halls of government itself. For the traitor appears not a traitor; he speaks in accents familiar to his victims, and he wears their face and their arguments, he appeals to the baseness that lies deep in the hearts of all men. He rots the soul of a nation, he works secretly and unknown in the night to undermine the pillars of the city, he infects the body politic so that it can no longer resist. A murderer is less to fear. The traitor is the plague." *Marcus Tullius Cicero, 58 B.C. Speech in the Roman Senate*

Contents:

Introduction

For generations the book of Revelation in the Bible has been coded with such symbolism that it's been very difficult to understand. Much of the source of that difficulty and interpretation has been because many words, situations, and conditions did not exist at the time Revelation was written. For example, words and descriptions such as: computers, airplanes, rockets, missiles and bombs did not exist at the time John did this writing. Although Christ gave John the visions of these things many did not have current descriptive words. Therefore, much is written with the best symbolism John could determine.

Now, in many cases, those descriptive words and symbols have no current reference points. Perhaps John didn't mean to code the words and descriptions as deeply as he did, but at that time he had no choice. For example, he couldn't have said, "All those missiles fired from ships offshore" if he didn't know there were ships offshore that could fire missiles that far. Likely he saw only the missiles falling when he wrote in 16:21, "And there fell upon men a great hail out of heaven, every stone about the weight of a talent: and men blasphemed God because of the plague of the hail; for the plague thereof was exceeding great." What could this mean in modern terms - during times of war?

The definition of a talent gives the major clue. Research indicates the weight of a talent has differed slightly throughout the ages, but it's normally suggested a talent is something that weighs from 57 to 130 pounds. At the time of the New Testament it was considered about 130 pounds, which is what John likely saw falling out of the sky; something weighing about 130 pounds. It's not unreasonable to understand that John saw artillery shells falling as hail from the sky. What other reasonable answer could exist? It's well acknowledged that a great war will happen at that time John described. Now, missiles and artillery shells are common elements of war.

Now, let's use this information as a basis and comparison for analyzing another statement in Revelation that's puzzled readers since it was written. A simple reading of the statement gives no clue as to its meaning; using the logic above presents a different conclusion. It makes the meaning crystal clear. Crystal clear means to see something or to understand something as it was meant to be - to understand the implication. Revelation begins with the introduction that what was to be written was seen by John. Verse 2 in the first chapter, speaking of John's role, states:

"Who bare record of the word of God, and of the testimony of Jesus Christ, and of all the things he saw." The phrase 'crystal clear' means the writings are pure and are to be interpreted, for they fulfill an important message.

What is the source of the comment, 'crystal clear?' Could it be from Chapter 4, Verse 6, "And before the throne there was a sea of glass like unto crystal; and in the midst of the throne, and round about the throne, were four beasts full of eyes before and behind." Is this Christ's way of saying 'I know all and can see all, in the past and in the future - before and behind?' Is his vision crystal clear?

Likely, this verse is to indicate the four beasts could see events 'behind' and into the future 'before.' This idea is further reinforced by Christ's instruction to John in Verse 19, "Write the things which thou hast seen, and the things which are, and the things which shall be hereafter." Is this not: behind; things in the past, and before; things

8

to come?

The description 'beast' does not describe an ugly horrible animal or a disfigured person. As in other parts of Revelation, it describes an entity or a condition. Christ tells us this in the first chapter of Revelation by explaining the meaning of candlesticks and stars. His explanation obviously is meant for that purpose.

This begins in Chapter 1, Verse 12, where John turns to see the voice that spoke behind him: "And I turned to see the voice that spake with me. And being turned, I saw seven golden candlesticks." Verse 16 adds, "And he had in his right hand seven stars." Christ explains that symbolism to John in Verse 20, "The mystery of the seven stars which thou sawest in my right hand, and the seven golden candlesticks. The seven stars are the angels of the seven churches: and the seven candlesticks which thou sawest are the seven churches." Then, in the letters to each of the seven churches, it's understood that the angels are the leaders of those churches; not necessarily angels as we visualize angels from Heaven. For example, it's similar to saying, "Your child is a perfect little angel."

After John's intervention with Christ, while John was 'in the spirit' and after Christ explained examples of symbolic meanings, then John was instructed to write certain things to each of the seven churches that were in an area identified as Asia at that time. Today, those ancient sites are located near each other in Western Turkey. The names of the current cities at those locations have changed, but some ruins of the old cities still exist at each location. The next chapter will describe the information presented to each of those churches in John's letters.

Understanding the introductory symbolism above will help better understand those letters. Perhaps that's why Christ gave that information to John when he first spoke to John and instructed him to write those letters. That information would not be clear and understood without that knowledge. The same for today. We are given a guide to read and understand Revelation. Since many people today have turned away from Christ, and many don't have a Bible; each of those seven letters will be presented in full to understand the symbolism.

Chapter 1
Seven Letters

Ephesus

The first letter John wrote from his vision was to Ephesus. Ephesus was the church where John had taught, and the location where he brought Mary, the mother of Jesus, after Jesus was crucified. It was also the church on the mainland of Asia closest to Patmos. John returned to Ephesus after he was released from his exile. The general guidance for the letters came from Chapter 1, Verse 19, "Write these things which thou hast seen, and the things which are, and the things which shall be hereafter." That letter to Ephesus begins:

"Unto the angel of the church of Ephesus write; These things saith he that holdeth the seven stars in his right hand, who walketh in the midst of the seven golden candlesticks; 2) I know thy works, and thy labor, and thy patience, and how thou canst bear them which are evil: and thou hast tried them which say they are apostles, and are not, and hast found them liars; 3) And hast borne, and hast patience, and for my name's sake hast laboured, and hast not fainted.

4) Nevertheless I have somewhat against thee, because thou hast left thy first love. 5) Remember therefore from whence thou art fallen, and repent, and do the first works; or else I will come unto thee quickly, and will remove thy candlestick out of his place, except thou

11

repent. 6) But this thou hast, that thou hatest the deeds of the Nicolaitanes, which I also hate." The letter concludes with a promise of salvation:

7) "He that hath an ear, let him hear what the Spirit saith unto the churches; To him that overcometh will I give to eat of the tree of life, which is in the midst of the paradise of God."

This letter begins by Christ explaining that he is the real and true Lord, the one who walks in the midst of the golden candlesticks. Then he praises them for working hard in his name and rejecting those who would lead them away from His word. Then he makes the first charge against those who 'say they are apostles and are not.' This is repeated in the letters to other churches. This is also the first indication that these letters are to all churches of all time, and not merely to the seven specified churches. Essentially, these letters are like the table of contents for things to come in the remainder of Revelation.

Reading later in Revelation, especially Chapters 6, 13 and 17, it becomes clear that the specification about those who 'say they are apostles, and are not' refers to Islam. Now, this is an unusual and unexpected statement to consider this early in Revelation, but as words in this book continue, it will become 'crystal clear.' First, it must be considered that during John's time no one would claim to be an apostle of Jesus who was not.

At that time followers of Jesus were sought out and killed, often by being crucified or beheaded. It would be illogical to consider people who would claim to be apostles who were not. That claim began in the mid 600s AD, when Muhammad claimed he was a prophet, on an order higher than Jesus. He was an apostle of a different order; an order of the antichrist.

However, although Muhammad was 'the' antichrist; he was not the only antichrist. As First John states in Verse 18, "Little children, it is the last time: and as ye have heard that antichirst shall come, even now are there many antichirsts; whereby we know that it is the last time." Although there have been many; perhaps the two most popular in recent history were Jim Jones and David Koresh.

Although Jim Jones never directly claimed to be Jesus; which is one of the definitions of an antichirst, neither did he ever deny it when asked. David Koresh claimed he was Jesus, and even went to Israel to find followers. And, there's another similarity among these three we might consider: Over 900 of Jones' followers died, most by suicide, in Jonestown, Guyana after a killing squad attacked and killed U.S. Congressman Leo Ryan at a nearby airport as Ryan was boarding to leave. David Koresh was one of 76 killed in the Mount Carmel Center near Waco, Texas after a long standoff with U.S. government agents in 1993. He was the leader of a group calling itself the Branch Davidians.

What is the similarity of these three? Revelation explains that millions of followers of the 'beast' will be killed during the great war, including the battle of Armageddon. Islam will be totally defeated; after many will be annihilated on the battlefield; as explained in Chapter 19, specifically Verse 21: "And the remnant were slain with the sword of him that sat on the horse, which sword proceeded out of his mouth: and all the fowls were filled with their flesh." A new and more peaceful world will arise when that happens. Followers of many other antichrists in the past have suffered the same deadly fate.

The letter to Ephesus also stated, "I have somewhat against thee, because thou hast left thy first love;" and then revealed a common hate of the Nicolaitanes. These two observations seem to have something in common - with a connection. In this admonition, perhaps Christ meant his followers at that church (and all churches of all time) should hold fast to his Word and not waver in their belief. This is explained in an article at Lightsource.com which gives the likely source of the word 'Nicolaitanes.' It suggests 'Nicolas'

13

wavered in his decisions about religious belief:

"Acts 6:5 tells us that this Nicolas was "a proselyte of Antioch." The fact that he was a proselyte tells us that he was not born a Jew but had converted from paganism to Judaism. Then he experienced a second conversion, this time turning from Judaism to Christianity. From this information, we know these facts about Nicolas of Antioch:

- He came from paganism and had deep pagan roots, very much unlike the other six deacons who came from a pure Hebrew line. Nicolas' pagan background meant that he had previously been immersed in the activities of the occult.

- He was not afraid of taking an opposing position, evidenced by his ability to change religions twice. Converting to Judaism would have estranged him from his pagan family and friends. It would seem to indicate that he was not impressed or concerned about the opinions of other people.

- He was a free thinker and very open to embracing new ideas and concepts. Judaism was very different from the pagan and occult world in which he had been raised. For him to shift from paganism to Judaism reveals that he was very liberal in his thinking, for most pagans were offended by Judaism. He was obviously not afraid to entertain or embrace new ways of thinking.

- When he converted to Christ, it was at least the second time he had converted from one religion to another. We don't know if, or how many times, he shifted from one form of paganism to another before he became a Jewish proselyte. His ability to easily change religious implies that he was not afraid to switch direction in midstream and go a totally different direction."

In summary, it seems the Nicolaitanes are those who cannot hold fast to their praise of God. To 'hold fast' is one of the great admonitions in Revelation. Nicolaitanes has another aspect of considering the body separate from the soul. That will be discussed in another section, since this idea is presented in more than one letter.

This letter to Ephesus concludes that those who remain faithful will 'eat of the tree of life.' This tree of life is explained later in Chapter 22, which begins: "And he shewed me a pure river of water of life, *clear as crystal*, proceeding out of the throne of God and of the Lamb. 2) In the midst of the street of it, and on either side of the river, was there the tree of life, which bare twelve manner of fruits, and yielded her fruit every month: and the leaves of the tree were for the healing of the nations."

What a great message presented in this first letter. This information says the world will still be here - in it's earthly form; and that the nations that will still exist as nations will be healed. The earth will not explode or be destroyed by a great fire. Mankind, if he or she chooses, may still walk barefoot upon earthly dirt.

Smyrna

John's second letter is to the church at Smyrna. It begins, "And unto the angel of the church in Smyrna write; These things saith the first and the last, which was dead, and is alive." In this verse, Christ explains the credibility and truth of his existence as opposed to those who claim his status; and those who claim they have taken his place with God. Then, the next verse shows the comparison; the difference:

Verse 9, "I know thy works, and tribulation, and poverty, (but thou art rich) and I know the blasphemy of them which say they are Jews, and are not, but are the synagogue of Satan." He begins by saying although they might have little physical assets, they are rich in the spirit of God. Those blessings make them rich. Then he repeats the charge that there are those who falsely claim they are Jews, as in descended from Jews.

Here, Christ changes the theme from false apostles in the first letter to false Jews in this letter to Smyrna. It's the same theme in different words for those who might not understand that different description of false claimants. In this case however, he moves closer to one of the major themes in Revelation. That theme is that Islam, the 'beast' is the major focus of Revelation. All is not revealed yet, but the analysis is getting closer. This case of false Jews refers to Islam's claim that they are descended from Jews; from Ishmael, the other son of Abraham, to give reference and credibility to their religion. It's been well documented to be a false claim. Verse 10 adds more:

"Fear none of those things which thou shalt suffer: behold, the devil shall cast some of you into prison, that ye may be tried; and ye shall have tribulation ten days: be thou faithful unto death, and I will give thee a crown of life."

This verse introduces two important events. First pertains to the tried or in some words, tested, for ten days. It's generally agreed by most reviewers that the time of ten days does not represent ten days as most would consider. Instead, it's another coded time for another event. And, since it involves time of hardship with a conclusion of possible death, this time is generally associated with that time known as the tribulation period. The tribulation will begin with the abomination of desolation; when the beast occupies Jerusalem, or the holy site in Jerusalem, and Jews flee from the city. Daniel 9:27 gives the description:

"And he (the beast) shall confirm the covenant with many for one week: and in the midst of the week he shall cause the sacrifice and the oblation to cease, and for the overspreading of abominations he shall make it desolate, even until the consummation, and that determined shall be poured upon the desolate." The times of ten days and one week seem confusing and integrated in these two referenced verses.

Let's examine further.

Many express the idea that this covenant is the same covenant as the current nuclear arms deal with Iran. Interesting that seven countries, including Iran, are involved with that covenant. Most concur that the one week, or seven days, actually means seven years because that more accurately gives a reasonable time line. Also, the length of the covenant, or agreement, with Iran is uncertain. The length of seven years, ten years, and fifteen years are all mentioned when one of those involved explains that agreement. The basic interpretation is that the covenant described in Daniel, and possibly the one with Iran at this time, is for seven years.

If seven years is the correct time of the covenant, then in three and a half years it will be abandoned by Iran, and at that time the tribulation will begin. Then the likely scenario is that Iran will suddenly attack, primarily Israel, and many will be jailed and or killed. Other nations might be peripherally involved, but Israel (Jerusalem) will be the initial and primary victim. The attack will be sudden.

Christ's other promise, "Be thou faithful unto death, and I will give thee a crown of life" is also explained further in Revelation. John writes in Chapter 20, Verse 4, "And I saw thrones, and they sat upon them, and judgment was given unto them: and I saw the souls of them that were beheaded for the witness of Jesus, and for the word of God, and which had not worshiped the beast, neither his image, neither had received his mark upon their foreheads, or in their hands; and they lived and reigned with Christ a thousand years." The next verse identifies this as the first resurrection. Verse 5 also states, "But the rest of the dead lived not again until the thousand years were finished."

Verse 11 repeats the common conclusion, "He that hath an ear, let him hear what the Spirit saith unto the churches; He that overcometh shall not be hurt of the second death." This second death refers to the judgment from the book of life for those who are not accepted in the first resurrection - all others.

Pergamos

The letter to Pergamos begins in Verse 12, still in Chapter 2: "And to the angel of the church in Pergamos write; These things saith he which hath the sharp sword with two edges; 13) I know they works, and where thou dwellest, even where Satan's seat is: and thou holdest fast my faith, even in those days wherein Antipas was my faithful martyr, who was slain among you, where Satan dwelleth." Although Verse 13 is very brief, it contains two important messages.

The first message regards 'Satan's seat.' Throughout the Bible Satan is represented many times by a serpent, even beginning in Genesis, in the Garden of Eden. This reference is to a snake that was brought to Pergamos and worshipped.

Pergamos, also called Pergamum by the Greeks, was the home of a famous medical center. It was dedicated to the Greek god of healing, named Asclepius. His symbol was the familiar serpent coiled on a staff that's still used today to represent medicine. The entrance to the medical center was decorated with a giant frieze of a serpent - which also represents Satan in the Bible. Hence, the 'seat of Satan.' Still, today, carved over the doorway are the words, "In the name of the gods, Death may not enter here." This great medical center was built by an Attalid prince named Archias who had gone to Greece to be healed of his wounds. He was so impressed with the great medical center in Greece he returned with medical priests to build the great center there in Pergamos.

The ruins of Pergamos   contain many artifacts, some still in wonderful condition, near the modern Turkish town of Bergama. The walls surrounding the ruins reach as far back as Pagan times, and many of the stones are intermingled from reuse over time. It has a theater which holds 3500 people and is still used for festivals, a gymnasium, a library, an alter of Aesculapius and several temples: Athena, Trajan, Dionysus, Hera and Zeus. It also has a sacred tunnel which is most unusual and still functional. Fodor's Turkey 1974 guide describes the ancient use of that tunnel.

"To the south, a two-storied portico makes up for a drop in the land. In the courtyard itself are traces of the sacred basins and the sacred spring of healing waters. Near the spring, a stairway goes downwards to a sacred tunnel, which the supplicants ran through after visiting the spring, while priests shouted words of encouragement from holes in the tunnel's roof. As they ran, they were told that the healing powers of the temple were taking effect, and that by the time they arrived at the round temple of Telesphorus, the god of cure-revealing dreams, they would be well again." This was part of the Aesclepion which had the serpent engraving symbolizing the 'seat of Satan.' Snakes were also in the sacred tunnel which participants ran through.

The current president, Barack Obama, also wears an adornment of this Satan symbol. His prized ring, which he has owned many years and even used it as his wedding ring, was once believed to be engraved with an Islamic symbol. Closer examination of his ring reveals that claim is untrue. Instead, his ring is adorned with two coiled serpents. This may be confirmed by anyone online by simply inquiring, 'Obama's ring.'

The next question in Verse 13 concerns Antipas. Who was he? During that time, many Christians were persecuted including an earlier leader of that church, Antipas. Antipas was killed by fire in a brazen bull, common at that earlier time. It was the same torture chamber into which Daniel's companions; Shadrach, Meshach and Abednego were cast, but survived with the hand of God protecting them. Seeing that their God had protected them from death, and seeing another man with them, King Nebuchadnezzar then gave them

19

words of praise; a promise to protect them against others, and promoted them to higher positions.

Antipas, on the other hand, suffered that horrible agony from which he did not deny God to escape; a true martyr. The unique quality of the brazen bull was that it was shaped so that a horrible sound would come from the mouth of the bull as the one inside moaned in agony before dying.

Verse 14 continues Christ's admonitions to Pergamos: "But I have a few things against thee, because thou hast there them that hold the doctrine of Balaam, who taught Balac to cast a stumbling block before the children of Israel, to eat things sacrificed unto idols, and to commit fornication." Verse 15 adds, "So has thou also them that hold the doctrine of the Nicolaitanes, which thing I hate." First, let's consider Ba'laam. This information is from a Prophesy Watch article:

"Balaam and Balac were introduced in Numbers 22. In that story, the Israelites had just left Egypt and had settled temporarily in Moab, where Balac was king. Observing Israelites as far as his eyes could see, Balac sent emissaries to get Balaam, 400 miles away, to come and put a curse on the Israelites. Balaam twice refused, saying God had not given him permission to do that. After Balac offered him more treasure, on the third try, and after God approved Balaam's trip, with instructions of what to say, Balaam began his journey. Along the way, Balaam's mule saw an angel standing in the way with a sword, and refused to advance. This resulted in a conversation between his mule and Balaam. Balaam eventually finished the trip into Moab to meet Balac. Balaam is mentioned in a negative tone in two other places:

Second Peter2:15 "Which have forsaken the right way, and are gone astray, following the way of Ba'laam the son of Bo'sor, who loved the way of unrighteousness."

Jude 11, "Woe unto them! For they have gone in the way of Cain, and ran greedily after the error of Ba'laam for reward, and perished in the gainsaying of Co're."

More information about Balaam is presented in 'The Prophecies of Balaam (Part One) by Richard T. Ritenbaugh Forerunner, "Prophecy Watch," February 2003:

"Balaam son of Beor is definitely an oddball among the prophets. He is not an Israelite but apparently a Syrian who lived in Pethor, a town situated near the Euphrates just south of Carchemish (Numbers 22:5). His prophecies result from an attempt to curse Israel in exchange for the money and honor of a frightened king of Moab, Balak son of Zippor (verses 2-7). To make matters worse, unlike any other prophet, he leads the Israelites into sin and brings a curse upon them, succeeding in getting 24,000 of them killed.

Since that time, his name has been a watchword denoting evil and avaricious character. As early as Deuteronomy 23:4-5, he is shown as an enemy of God and Israel and degraded as a hired mercenary. Joshua positively notes his death at the hand of Israelites (Joshua 13:22), and he also repeats Balaam's overthrow by God in a list of His victories for Israel (Joshua 24:9-10). Nehemiah and Micah recall him to the people of their days as an evil man whom God defeated (Nehemiah 13:2; Micah 6:5).

The New Testament mentions Balaam three times, all negatively. Both Peter and Jude describe him as the personification of greed in using religion for personal gain (II Peter 2:15; Jude 11). Revelation 2:14 credits him with "the doctrine of Balaam," which is inducing others to sin, specifically to idolatry and sexual immorality." End of Prophesy Watch article.

The doctrine of Nicolaitanes was discussed earlier. It involves the doctrine of separating the spirit from the body; whereby the spirit

21

could be accepted for salvation regardless of the sins of the body. This is the second time Christ addressed this and said He hated it.

Now, since this is combined with the teachings by Balaam of sexual immorality, another conclusion may be made of the doctrine of Nicolaitines; it would include homosexuality. It's that concept of considering the body and soul separate; so that one's body might commit homosexual acts - which Christ hates; but yet believe the soul might still be saved. Leviticus and Romans give much more description and explanation of sexual immorality, homosexuality, and fornication.

The letter adds in Verse 17, "He that hath an ear, let him hear what the Spirit saith unto the churches; To him that overcometh will I give to eat of the hidden manna, and will give him a white stone, and in the stone a new name written, which no man knoweth saving he that receiveth it. " The hidden manna, of course, is that from the 'tree of life' described in Chapter 22, Verse 2. The 'white stone' is the symbol of approval, versus the black stone which is the symbol of denial; or guilt. In this, Christ suggests that those who are approved with the white stone understand the meaning of that approval - they have accepted the Spirit of God into their souls; while those who don't understand cannot accept God's Spirit to have that understanding.

Thyatira

The letter to the church at Thyatira begins in Verse 18 of Chapter 2, "And unto the church in Thyatira write; These things saith the Son of God, who hath his eyes like unto a flame of fire, and his feet are like fine brass; 19) I know thy works, and charity, and service, and faith, and thy patience, and thy works; and the last to be more than the first.

This letter begins with an affirmation that the one creating the vision and the information is the true one; the true Son of God. He adds that his vision is pure because he has the power to see all things as if they were being burned with fire. And, his feet are powerful enough to endure all things with his everlasting life; the most vicious torture chambers of that day were brass bulls. In this, Christ was announcing that his words and strength were powerful; not like others who would falsely claim to be God's prophet. Christ's words also praised those at Thyatira because their more recent works had improved since the beginning of their acceptance of Christ's word and they had spread the word of God. Then, Verse 20 takes a different turn - an admonition:

"Notwithstanding, I have a few things against thee, because thou sufferest that woman Jezebel, which calleth herself a prophetess, to teach and to seduce my servants to commit fornication, and to eat things sacrificed unto idols." To understand this verse, it's first necessary to understand the use of the term 'woman.'

Heretofore, many have tried to interpret its meaning as literally 'a woman.' That's not what this verse really means. To interpret the meaning we must first analyze the use of the term woman in Chapters 12 and 17. The word woman, as used here, refers to a religion; not to a person. This will be analyzed later, but will be briefly explained here, to understand the intent of this letter.

Chapter 12 introduces the first woman that represents Christianity. It begins, "And there appeared a great wonder in heaven; a woman clothed with the sun, and the moon under her feet, and upon her head a crown of twelve stars." Verse 2 adds, "And she being with child cried, travailing in birth, and pained to be delivered." Verse 3 describes another wonder in heaven. Notice this is not a 'great' wonder. Verse 4 describes the intent of that 'dragon,' "And the dragon stood before the woman which was ready to be delivered, for to devour her child as soon as it was born."

The remainder of Chapter 12 further describes that woman, Christianity, and the enmity of the dragon against her and the remnant of her seed. The most descriptive entry is Verse 14, which describes the time Christianity is protected by Rome, 'two wings of a great eagle' for three hundred and fifty years. That's when the next woman arose to renew the attack against the first woman, Christianity. After 350 years of persecution, then another 350 years of acceptance and protection under Rome carried the time to 700 AD. That's when Islam was established. Muhammad's attack on Christians (the remnant of her seed) began in the mid 600s.

Islam is the second woman in Revelation. Most information about this woman is found in Chapter 17; after being introduced by the entry in the letter to Thyatira and by the introduction of the rider of the red horse in 6:4. This reference in Chapter 6 describes a rider who will take peace from the earth and will 'kill one another.' This describes the two parts of Islam. Those two parts are detailed further in 17:5 as Babylon and her harlot. Their 'killing one another' is detailed in 17:16.

How do we know this is the same rider who will kill one another? Chapter 6 describes the one rider on the red horse. Chapter 17 describes the woman in 17:3 as riding the scarlet horse. Now, how do we know this woman riding the red horse, also the scarlet horse represents Islam? Because 17:6 describes her as 'the woman drunken with the blood of the saints and with the blood of the martyrs of Jesus.' Considering the time sequences given, this woman, Islam, is the only one who has consistently made war with the remnant of her seed and been drunken with the blood of Christians.

So, we now return to the woman Jezebel, who is fully described as the religion Islam. The questions regarding fornication and eating food sacrificed to idols is now answered. Their halal food is that food sacrificed to idols; the black cube in Mecca that houses an ancient pagan relic - a black meteorite stone. Worship of that stone was a ritual of pagan moon god worshipers; from which Islam was derived. Have you noticed the crescent moon that symbolizes Islam and adorns many of their mosques? That's the source of that symbol.

And about her fornication? That's answered in 17:4, "...having a golden cup in her hand full of abominations and filthiness of her fornication." Then the letter continues with more information about that woman, Islam. Verses 21-22 add: "And I gave her space to repent of her fornications, and she repented not. Behold, I will cast her into a bed, and them that commit adultery with her into great tribulation, except they repent of their deeds." These verses are also expanded and explained in Chapters 17-18.

More background information is given in Chapter 17 which leads to more answers in Chapter 18. For example, what was in that 'golden cup?' 18:3 explains: "For all nations have drunk of the wine of the wrath of her fornication, and the kings of the earth have committed fornication with her, and the merchants of the earth are waxed rich through the abundance of her delicacies." And since 'she repented not' the judgment is identified in 18:5, "For her sins have reached unto heaven, and God hath remembered her iniquities."

Then more information is written in the letter that matches information expanded in Chapter 17 and the remainder of Revelation. Remember; this was written approximately 700 years before Islam became established. In that letter, Verse 23 announces God's judgment against Islam: "And, I will kill her children with death; and all the churches shall know that I am he which searcheth the reins and hearts: and I will give unto every one of you according to your works." Those deaths are explained later in Revelation:

First, is the death from the two divisions of Islam; as is happening even now is the Islamic world. The two heads; Islam and radical Islam, the Sunni and the Shiite are slaughtering each other by the thousands in the Middle East. This is prophesied in 17:16-17, "And

25

the ten horns (Islamic countries) which thou sawest upon the beast, these shall hate the whore (the harlot radicals) and shall make her desolate, and naked, and shall eat her flesh, and burn her with fire. 17) For God hath put in their hearts to fulfil his will..."

Second, Chapter 19 explains the great battle after which the beast and the false prophet, Verse 20, were taken and, "These both were cast alive into a lake of fire burning with brimstone." Then Verse 21 explains what happens to those remaining also to be killed, "And the remnant were slain with the sword of him that sat upon the horse (the white horse) which sword proceeded out of his mouth: and all fowls were filled with their flesh." Of course, God will not physically kill those with a sword; but instead will guide his followers and believers in that process 'with the sword of his mouth.'

Verse 24 begins a positive promise of things to come for those who believe; and it's also a reminder that this is the true Christ and not the false one who claims to take his place, that prophetess Jezebel. "But unto you I say, and unto the rest in Thyatira, as many as have not this doctrine, and which have not known the depths of Satan, as they speak; I will put upon you none other burden. 25) But that which ye have already hold fast till I come. 26) And he that overcometh, and keepeth my works unto the end, to him will I give the power over the nations."

Verse 27 continues: "And he shall rule them with a rod of iron; as the vessels of a potter shall they be broken to shivers: even as I received my Father. 28) And I will give him the morning star. 29) He that hath an ear hear what the Spirit sayeth unto the churches." Two things are important in these last verses. First, is the promise of the 'morning star.' This is mentioned in other places in Revelation, and seems to suggest the continuing presence of Christ and the Spirit. Second, is that the last verse references churches; not just the seven churches. This would include the churches of our time, and even beyond.

Sardis

The letter to Sardis is different from the other letters. It's purpose seems to be an overall warning to hold fast to the faith, because one never knows the exact time of judgment. It begins: "And unto the angel of the church in Sardis write: These things saith he that hath the seven Spirits of God, and the seven stars; I know thy works, that thou hast a name, that thou livest, and art dead. Verse 2, "Be watchful, and strengthen the things which remain, that are ready to die: for I have not found thy works perfect before God." This seems a reminder that those alive have a name that will later be judged from the book of life. It's also a warning that the time might come when one might have to make the decision not to reject God, when faced with the possibility of death.

Verse 3 continues: "Remember therefore how thou hast received and heard, and hold fast, and repent. If therefore thou shalt not watch, I will come on thee as a thief, and thou shalt not know what hour I will come upon thee. 4) Thou hast a few names even in Sardis which have not defiled their garments; and they shall walk with me in white: for they are worthy." Clothed in white is a common phrase to identify those who hold fast to the Word of God. It's very significant in two other places in Revelation:

One is in 7:11, where the souls of those waiting to be redeemed are given white robes while they waited for the second resurrection. They were told "that they should rest yet for a little season, until their fellowservants also and their brethren, that should be killed, as they were, should be fulfilled." Those to be killed referred to those beheaded because they would refuse the mark of the beast described in Chapter 13. Those killed for refusing the mark of the beast would be resurrected first in what's described as the first resurrection. The others would have to wait until after the prophesied thousand years.

Another mention of clothed in white is from 19:14, where God's army is prepared for battle, "And the armies which were in heaven followed him upon white horses, clothed in fine linen, white and clean." Verse 5 begins the promise of salvation:

"He that overcometh, the same shall be clothed in white raiment; and I will not blot out his name out of the book of life, but I will confess his name before my Father, and before his angels." Verse 6 is the common reminder to all churches, "He that hath an ear, let him hear what the Spirit saith unto the churches."

Philadelphia

This letter begins in Chapter 3, Verse 7: "And to the angel of the church in Philadelphia write; These things saith he that is holy, he that is true, he that hath the key of David, he that openeth, and no man shutteth; and shutteth, and no man openeth; 8) I know thy works: behold, I have set before thee an open door, and no man can shut it: for thou hast a little strength, and hast kept my word, and hast not denied my name." Again, in this letter Christ is saying and affirming that he is the true Son of God, and not an imposter; he has the real key of David. After he commends his followers for not being persuaded to believe those other than himself, he then mentions those who are imposters in the next verse, 9:

"Behold, I will make them of the synagogue of Satan, which say they are Jews, and are not, but do lie; behold, I will make them to come and worship before thy feet, and to know that I have loved thee." As in previous letters, Christ is warning of imposters; those who claim to be sent in place of Christ, or those who themselves claim to be Christ; and those who worship them. They claim to be descended from Jews to bolster their claim of a valid religion.

The greatest incident of this type to occur, of course, is the claim by

Muhammad that he is the true prophet; instead of Christ. This claim by Muhammad, in itself, identifies Muhammad as the antichrist discussed in other parts of the Bible. In Revelation, only the term 'beast' is used to identify this person. Muhammad, himself, never claimed to be descended from Jews, but those who bolstered his claim of that religion falsely pretended he was descended from Jews in the lineage of Abraham and Ishmael. This link provides one information source that it's a false claim:

http://religionresearchinstitute.org/mohammad/ishmael.htm

The next four verses, 10-13, again encourage his followers to hold fast and not abandon their belief; to keep their names in the book of life:

"Because thou hast kept the word of my patience, I also will keep thee from the hour of temptation, which shall come upon all the world, to try them that dwell upon the earth. 11) Behold, I come quickly: hold that fast which thou hast, that no man take thy crown. 12) Him that overcometh will I make a pillar in the temple of my God, and he shall go no more out: and I will write upon him the name of my God, and the name of the city of my God, which is new Jerusalem, which cometh down out of heaven from my God: and I will write upon him my new name. 13) He that hath an ear, let him hear what the Spirit saith unto the churches."

Laodicea

The letter to the church at Laodicea begins in Verse 14, "And unto the angel of the church of the Laodiceans write; These things saith the Amen, the faithful and true witness, the beginning of the creation of God;" Again, to differentiate himself from the imposters, those who claim they are Jews and are not, Christ makes it very clear who he is and why his Word must be believed. The letter continues, "I know thy works, that thou art neither cold nor hot: I would thou wert cold or hot.16) So then because thou art lukewarn, and neither cold nor hot, I will spue thee out of my mouth." This metaphor will be explained below. The letter continues:

Verse 17, "Because thou sayest, I am rich, and increased with goods, and have need of nothing; and knowest not that thou are wretched, and miserable, and poor, and blind, and naked: 18) I counsel thee to buy of me gold tried in the fire, that thou mayest be rich; and white raiment; that thou mayest be clothed, and that the shame of thy nakedness do not appear; and anoint thine eyes with eyesalve, that thou mayest see."

Verse 19 continues, "As many as I love, I rebuke, and chasten; be zealous therefore, and repent. 20) Behold, I stand at the door, and knock: if any man hear my voice, and open the door, I will come in to him, and have sup with him, and he with me. 21) To him that overcometh will I grant to sit with me in my throne, even as I also overcame, and am set down with my Father in his throne." Verse 22 repeats the common caution: "He that hath an ear, let him hear what the Spirit saith unto the churches."

Many have used the term 'neither hot nor cold' from this reading to the church of Laodicea. For Laodicea, these words have not only a symbolic meaning, they also express a real and physical meaning for that location. The written words clearly mean that those in the church were not truly dedicated to the faith; to the Spirit of God. They observed Christianity only as a normal and passing event or idea; perhaps similar to many who claim to be Christians today. The physical aspects of hot nor cold are simpler to explain.

Ruins of the ancient city of Hierapolis are about ten miles away from the ancient cite of Laodicea. It's located in a flat plain below a mountain upon which sits the ancient city Hierapolis. Located there with Hierapolis is an ancient Roman resort, named Pamukkale. This is a short description from Wikipedia:

"Pamukkale, meaning 'cotton castle' in Turkish, is a natural site in Denizli Province in southwestern Turkey. The city contains hot springs and travertines, terraces of carbonate minerals left by the flowing water. It is located in Turkey's Inner Aegean region, in the River Menderes valley, which has a temperate climate for most of the year.

The ancient Greco-Roman and Byzantine city of Hierapolis was built on top of the white "castle" which is in total about 2,700 metres (8,860 ft) long, 600 m (1,970 ft) wide and 160 m (525 ft) high. It can be seen from the hills on the opposite side of the valley in the town of Denizli, 20 km away.

Tourism is and has been a major industry. People have bathed in its pools for thousands of years. As recently as the mid-20th century, hotels were built over the ruins of Hierapolis, causing considerable damage. An approach road was built from the valley over the terraces, and motor bikes were allowed to go up and down the slopes. When the area was declared a World Heritage Site, the hotels were demolished and the road removed and replaced with artificial pools. Wearing shoes in the water is prohibited to protect the deposits."

The natural pools at the top of the mountain were hot, which provided great relaxation for Romans; and many before and after them, still even today. The hot waters had a natural flow down to the flat plain below, where Laodicea was located. When it reached Laodicea, it was only lukewarm; neither hot nor cold. The natural water also provided much riches for the area, for which they were criticized in John's letter.

Laodicea was located on a major trade crossroads, and from its great natural water flow had sufficient grain and other foods to grow livestock, in particular a special sheep that produced a greatly desired

black wool. The sheep also produced an oil that was special to make important eye salves; forming the basis of the comment in John's letter, "and anoint thine eyes with eyesalve, that thou mayest see."
.

The caution in Verse18, "I counsel thee to buy of me gold tried in the fire, that thou mayest be rich; and white raiment; that thou mayest be clothed, and that the shame of thy nakedness do not appear;" also refers to the idea that they were rich in assets and not in Spirit, and that they were clothed (made wealthy) from wool, and not from what should be their first love. Clothed in white raiment has already been explained in a previous letter. God, and those 'dressed in white raiment' will defeat the Devil and his beasts in that final great battle.

Hierapolis was the home of Philip the Evangelist. Thirteen miles away is the ancient city of Colossae, where Paul wrote the letters to the Colossians. In his letter he mentioned Laodicea two times:

Chapter 2, First verse: "For I would that ye knew what great conflict I have for you, and for them at Laodicea, and for as many as have not seen my face in the flesh."

Chapter 4, verse 13: "For I bear him record, that he hath a great zeal for you, and them that are in Laodicea and them in Hierapolis."

My wife and I enjoyed the warmth of the pools as our two children splashed and played in the waters on Pamukkale, where we stayed overnight in a small hotel. Unsure of the food, we drank the local wine and ate the local bread called ekmek, which was handed to us unwrapped, which is normal. It also had to be eaten almost immediately, or else it became too hard to eat.

While we relaxed in the warm water and watched our children splash about playing in the pool, we wondered if the ancient Romans enjoyed the water, the hot water that became lukewarm when it reached Laodicea, the same way. As perhaps did many ancient

Romans, we returned several times to Pamukkale.

Conclusion

Perhaps the warning to these seven churches to pay attention to events and listen to what the Spirit sayeth was not just for the seven churches. Too often the admonishment was repeated, "He that hath an ear" pay attention to what's happening - to current reality. It was repeated, and emphasized, for each of those churches - for every church. We are also told elsewhere in the Bible that when two or more people meet in God's name; there is a church. Therefore, we don't have to set foot inside a building called a church to be warned.

At this time, and from these churches; what is our greatest warning from God in the Book of Revelation? To watch and to understand what's happening around us. Three things were emphasized over and over: To hold fast to our faith in Christ; To beware that Jezebel who will lead many astray; To avoid sexual immorality and fornication.

He introduced us to that woman, Jezebel, as being in the church at Thyatira; but He didn't say who she was, and He didn't say she was not in other churches. Later, in Chapter 17, He showed us exactly who that Jezebel, religion, is. It's clearly the Islamic religion "drunken with the blood of the saints and with the blood of the martyrs of Jesus." That description could not be more clear and definitive.

This woman, this religion, didn't exist until seven hundred years after the letters were written to the seven churches. There would have been no way for those in the seven churches at that time to interpret what the letters mean today. The letters were warnings for future events to occur.

We are warned not to be seduced by that prophetess. Those who fall into her trap, or blindly turn aside and accept her ways, will be denied their salvation with God. That's why the Seven Spirits of God are within us; for power to defeat that great Beast and her Red Dragon.

And, we were warned to refrain from sexual immorality and fornication. In this warning, He spoke to individuals, churches, and nations as shown in Leviticus 18:24, "Defile not ye yourselves in any of these things; for in all these the nations are defiled which I cast out before you."

The children of Israel suffered His wrath for many generations when He cast them out of their land when they turned against his Word. Should we in the United States, or any other part of the world, consider ourselves safe from His wrath and His promises just because we consider ourselves more important, more worldly, and more sophisticated than the ancient Jews? He has given us the strength, the Seven Spirits, to overcome these daily pressures. Those will be discussed next.

Chapter 2
The Seven Spirits

Introduction

For those unaware, the Bible's book of Revelation was written by the apostle John who was exiled on the Island of Patmos, which is just off the western side of Turkey. When John wrote Revelation, that area was considered Asia. John wrote seven letters to what was at that time the seven churches in Asia Minor. John's words to the seven churches, and the writings that followed, were given to him by Christ in a vision. John's writing says the words were written as they were given to him. Placed many times in John's writing is the mention of the seven Spirits of God. The first mention is in 1:4:

"John to the seven churches which are in Asia; Grace be unto you, and peace, from him which is, and which was, and which is to come; and from the seven Spirits which are before his throne." This is the first introduction of the 'seven Spirits.' There is no suggestion or indication what they are or what they might be. Christ is the one John references as 'which is, and was, and which is to come,' referring to his birth, death, and his return as the Messiah in the future. Those seven Spirits are also coded, and I will reveal them as soon as I put some of the other pieces together where they might have more understanding and meaning.

The seven Spirits of God; what are they? After they are introduced in reference 1:4, above, their mention continues as an integral part throughout Revelation:

3:1, And unto the angel of the church in Sardis write; These things saith he that hath the seven Spirits of God, and the seven stars; I know thy works, that thou has a name, that thou livist, and art dead.

3:6, 3:13, 3:22: He that hath an ear, let him hear what the Spirit saith unto the churches.

4:2, And immediately I was in the Spirit: and, behold, a throne was set in heaven, and one sat on the throne.

4:5, And out of the throne proceeded lightnings and thunderings and voices; and there were seven lamps of fire burning before the throne, which are the seven Spirits of God.

5:6, And I beheld, and, lo, in the midst of the throne and of the four beasts, and in the midst of the elders, stood a Lamb as it had been slain, having seven horns and seven eyes, which are the seven Spirits of God sent forth into all the earth.

5:12, Saying with a loud voice, Worthy is the Lamb that was slain to receive power, and riches, and wisdom, and strength, and honour, and glory, and blessings."

It seems some important information is scattered and coded in Revelation, and when placed in a certain order seems to give a clearer message, although still not perfectly clear as would be stated in current language. In this case, it seems the seven Spirits are very important in God's realm. They are mentioned several times in key positions, and all those positions seem interrelated.

Reference 5:12 says the Lamb, Jesus, was slain to receive those seven things. The earlier reference 5:6 says the Lamb had those seven Spirits of God sent forth into all the world. Into "all the world" must mean the world of believers. If God and Jesus already had those things just for themselves why would they send them into all the world if not for other people, believers, to be influenced by them or use them. Simply, they would serve no other purpose except to be acknowledged and or used. The questions: do we acknowledge those seven Spirits given to us, and how are we prepared to use them?

Perhaps John's written statement in 4:2 gives a condition that must exist before one can receive the seven Spirits. "And immediately I was in the Spirit: and, behold, a throne was set in heaven, and one sat on the throne." What is the clue to receiving those seven Spirits? John's statement that he was in the Spirit would suggest that to receive something from God, one must be in the Spirit of God. Perhaps this implies, or strongly purports, that one must be a believer to allow a channel to receive those gifts, including the gifts of the seven Spirits. Perhaps they should be explored separately and individually? Power is the first Spirit acknowledged in reference 5:12, so let's consider how power could be one of the Spirits given to us, and what it might suggest.

Power

There are many viewpoints from which to consider the word 'power.' The first that ordinarily comes to mind is physical might or force; having the power to overcome some physical force or obstacle. But, a physical power initiated against another person or another religion or thought would be totally contrary to God's teaching. In Godliness, we should never initiate physical force, or power, against another. So - what could be the meaning of this power expressed in John's writings? Could it be the power of words, actions and deeds? Could it be something possessed individually, or in a group? Could the answer be - both? And, could there be an important exception as in war?

Clearly there's an intrinsic power in the mere acceptance of the Christian idea. The Words of God, the sacrifice of Jesus, and the Spirit that binds true Christians together form that power. Others, the non-believers and others who attack the Spirit of that power, are fearful of the belief in that Spirit. For those, the Spirit that binds Christians together is a force of power they don't understand; and since they don't understand it or refuse to accept it, it's a force that must be destroyed. It's a power that binds humanity; a power that prevents anarchy and destruction of human benevolence.

It's the power that represents the significance of humans in the realm of God and His creation. That universal power of the 'church' is necessary to maintain its existence. Those refusing to acknowledge the Spirit are guided and influenced by worldliness and physical things they can only see and touch; and perhaps with a touch of recognition of their fellow man; within limitations. There is no common relationship that binds them to the existence of life other than what they see and feel. They refuse to let the Spirit enter into their beings so they may feel part of the greater creation. Although not clearly or totally connected, two other verses in Revelation are references that might explain this power concept even further. They are Chapter 2, Verse 26, and Chapter 20, Verse 4:

Chapter 2, Verse 26: "And he that overcometh, and keepeth my works unto the end, to him will I give power over the nations;" The next verse explains further, but is certainly more cryptic.

Chapter 20, Verse 4: "And I saw thrones, and they sat upon them, and judgment was given unto them: and I saw the souls of them that were beheaded for the witness of Jesus, and for the word of God and which had not worshiped the beast, neither his image, neither had received his mark upon their foreheads, or in their hands; and they lived and reigned with Christ a thousand years."

The reference in Chapter 2 directly points to the use of power. The reference in Chapter 20 suggests the final use of that power. Of course, many verses in Revelation refer to other conditions or situations that occur before or after the referenced verse, as do these two references.

The first reference, Chapter 2, has a clearer meaning and more understanding after reading two later verses in Chapter 22. Verse 2 refers to the healing of the nations; those nations mentioned in the first reference. The comment, "And he that overcometh, and keepeth my works unto the end..." have more clarity after reading verse 7 in Chapter 22; "Behold, I come quickly: blessed is he that keepeth the sayings of the prophecy of this book."

The verse in Chapter 20 referring to "the souls of them that were beheaded" refers back to Chapter 13. This chapter gives specific information about the beast (the antichrist) and the second beast (the false prophet.) In this reference, the second beast causes mankind to worship an image of the antichrist and to have a mark upon themselves to buy and sell; known as the 'mark of the beast.' According to the reference, those who refuse to worship the beast or accept the mark will be killed - beheaded.

There is some confusion in this phrasing and in another reference that addresses the thousand years, often called the 'Millennium,' when those raised up will rule with God in Heaven. Some interpret this as the time of 'Rapture' when the last believers on earth will be swept away and disappear into Heaven - avoiding the time of great tribulation. This is the basis of the 'Left Behind' series of articles. The idea that people will suddenly disappear from earth 'leaving others behind' is totally fallacious according to scripture. The word or the concept of the rapture does not exist in the Bible. This misinterpretation is from the concept of the first resurrection and the second resurrection.

The first resurrection will be for the souls of those killed and beheaded for refusing to worship the image of the beast or to accept his mark. Only these souls will be carried away - resurrected - at this time. Their bodies will not be included in something called the rapture by those who don't understand the full meaning of the first resurrection and the second resurrection. The second resurrection will be for all others, before and after the thousand years Satan is locked away, below, in the pits of fire.

Does that spirit, Power, really exist? Can believers who have been blessed with it actually feel it within themselves? How is it manifested otherwise?

Christians who have accepted the Word of God know this power; they understand it and they feel it. It's something that glows within their character as others see them and watch them. Although others might claim they are foolish and uninformed in their belief, nevertheless they watch and listen in awe as a real Christian walks in God's light. It's an unseen and unspoken power that expresses God's glory. This power shines so brightly that it must be destroyed by others who follow the persuasions of a 'strange' god. Who is this strange god, and where did he come from? This strange god was identified in Daniel, Chapter 11, Verses 38 and 39. In these verses, Daniel is speaking of the Beast, also known in other parts of the Bible as the Antichrist.

Verse 38: "But in his estate shall he honour the God of forces: and a god whom his fathers knew not shall he honour with gold, and silver, and with precious stones, and pleasant things."

Verse 39: "Thus shall he do in the most strong holds with a strange god, whom he shall acknowledge and increase with glory: and he shall cause them to rule over many, and shall divide the land for gain."

Daniel wrote this 500 years before Christ was born. Muslims didn't discover their god until 600 years after Christ was born. When Daniel wrote this, any god unknown at his time would be a strange god - would it not? The Islamists' god is the only one unknown when Daniel wrote this information.

This strange god, as introduced by Daniel, is the only one who forms a basis for the destruction of Christians, and others who refuse to worship their god. Accordingly, the followers of that strange god are compelled to kill Christians - behead them - to destroy that power they possess from God. Would a god who commanded the destruction and death of others by bloodletting not be a strange god in any universe that recognizes any god?

So, how does this strange god fit into the pattern of humanity described in the Book of Revelation? Perhaps the description, and the understanding of the two women introduced in Revelation will help explain this question. It concerns war and bloodletting.

The prophesy about the continuing war on Christians today is clear - and without doubt. Chapter 12; Verse 17 is very specific and needs little interpretation: "And the dragon was wroth with the woman, and went to make war with the remnant of her seed, which keep the commandments of God, and have the testimony of Jesus Christ." It's this power, this Spirit, that grants followers to defend against this powerful danger. And, they must have strength to use that power. Strength is the next Spirit identified in that list.

Strength

This quote from Chapter 17 suggests why the spirit of Strength is necessary for Christians and Jews to 'hold fast' to the true Word. There are other references in Revelation that indicate many Jewish people will accept Christ in their Jewish belief. Specifically, 144,000 will be converted; 12,000 from each of the 12 tribes.

Certainly, Jewish people who worship God, and refuse to accept Jesus as the Messiah will also be given the spirit of Strength to persevere through these difficult times. Everyone who worships God will be challenged in those final days of prophesy. According to John's writing, that other woman, that religion, will be very appealing. This is how John described that appeal of Islam:

"And there came one of the seven angels which had the seven vials, and talked with me, saying unto me, Come hither; I will shew unto thee the judgement of the great whore that sitteth upon many waters;"

Verse 4 continues: "...a golden cup in her hand full of abominations and filthiness of her fornication:"

Verse 5 adds, "And upon her forehead was a name written, MYSTERY, BABYLON THE GREAT, THE MOTHER OF HARLOTS AND ABOMINATIONS OF THE EARTH."

Verse 6 is clear and indisputable. It describes exactly who the second woman (religion) is - the one that will wage war against Christians and Jews in that great war. "And I saw the woman drunken with the blood of the saints, and with the blood of the martyrs of Jesus: and when I saw her, I wondered with great admiration."

The angel was puzzled by John's reaction and acceptance of the woman with great admiration. In the next verse, the angel asked: "And the angel said unto me, Wherefore didst thy marvel? I will tell thee the mystery of the woman, and of the beast that carrieth her, which hath the seven heads and ten horns."

Verse 8 adds: "The beast that thou sawest was, and is not; and shall ascend out of the bottomless pit, and into perdition;..." Verse 11 repeats this identification:

"And the beast that was, and is not, even he is the eighth, and is of the seven, and goeth into perdition."

Now, let's pause and consider the angel's description of the religion that will be "drunken with the blood of the saints, and with the blood of the martyrs of Jesus." Presently, and throughout recent history, only those guided by the Islamic faith have consistently spilled the blood of Christians and Jews. Many of their writings and traditions require them to make the world pure; that purity being a world that is totally Islamic without tolerance for any person of any other religion to live. The most basic traditions of their leaders require those who do not accept their god to be killed - particularly by beheading. And, in the most extreme cases, it doesn't matter if those they kill and behead are men, women, or children.

Since it's so self-evident that Islamists continue that slaughter of innocents throughout the world today, an appropriate question is in order. That question is: Who set the example for Muslims to kill others not of the Muslim faith simply because they do not accept that faith? It began with Muhammad himself.

TheReligionofPeace.com presented an article disputing the myth that Muhammad waged war and attacks on others, especially Christians and Jews, only for defensive purposes. According to this article and many others, Muhammad often led unprovoked and unwarranted attacks. This is part of that article. The given references are from Islamic documents:

"One of the best documented examples of Muslim aggression during the lifetime of Muhammad is the attack on the peaceful community of Khaybar. This followed the treaty of Hudaibiya between the Muslims and Meccans, which called for a period of peace between the two groups. The treaty was controversial with Muslims, not only because it contradicted Allah's prior mandate to "drive out" the Meccans with violent force (2:191), but also because Muhammad agreed not to be recognized as a prophet in the document (Muslim 4401).

Muhammad decided that it was prudent to attack the Jews at Khaybar in order to regain the respect of his people and placate their grumbling with military victory and (especially) the stolen wealth that followed. This is embarrassing to modern-day Muslim apologists, who try to justify the siege by imagining that the sleepy farming community, located about 100 miles outside of Medina, posed some sort of necessary threat.

Unfortunately for contemporary apologists, not only is there no supporting evidence that the Muslims were under attack by the Khaybar, there are at least three historical references that flatly contradict any notion of self-defense on the part of Muhammad. The first is a description of the initial attack by Ibn Ishaq/Hisham:

'We met the workers of Khaybar coming out in the morning with their spades and baskets. When they saw the apostle and the army they cried, "Muhammad with his force," and turned tail and fled...' The apostle seized the property piece by piece... (Ibn Ishaq/Hisham 757)

The people of Khaybar were not attacking Muhammad. They were farming their land with shovels and buckets, not even knowing that they were supposed to be at war. This is further confirmed in the same text:

'When the apostle raided a people he waited until the morning. If he heard a call to prayer he held back; if he did not hear it he attacked. We came to Khaybar by night, and the apostle passed the night there; and when morning came he did not hear the call to prayer, so he rode and we rode with him.' (Ibn Ishaq/Hisham 757)

Muhammad attacked only after waiting to see if the people of

Khaybar issued a morning call to prayer. This would have no possible relevance had they already been at war with him.

Perhaps the best proof that Muhammad was not acting in self-defense is the fact that his own people did not understand why they were marching to war. His son-in-law, who was in charge of the military expedition, had to ask for justification:

'Allah's Messenger called Ali [and said]: "Proceed on and do not look about until Allah grants you victory," and Ali went a bit and then halted and did not look about and then said in a loud voice: "Allah's Messenger, on what issue should I fight with the people?" Thereupon he (the Prophet) said: "Fight with them until they bear testimony to the fact that there is no god but Allah and Muhammad is his Messenger..." (Sahih Muslim 5917)

The question Ali posed would have been unnecessary had the Muslims been under attack by the Khaybar or if the answer to the question were obvious. As it is, Muhammad's reply underscores the ostensible purpose of the campaign, which was to force the Jews into acknowledging the superiority of Islam.

Muhammad's men easily captured Khaybar and divided up the loot. The prophet of Islam tortured the community's treasurer to extract information, then had him killed (Ibn Ishaq/Hisham 764). Muhammad then took the man's widow, Saffiya, as his wife after trading two other captured women to one of his lieutenants (Ibn Ishaq/Hisham 758). The surviving Jews were allowed to stay on their land provided that they gave their Muslim masters an ample share of their crops.

Therefore, the rule of aggression in Islam, from the example set by Muhammad, is that it is proportional to the power held by Muslims, and not the persecution that they are under. The rare verses of peace in the Qur'an were "revealed" in Mecca, when true oppression existed (in some cases). The verses of violence that are revealed later correspond to Muslim military might even as any persecution of Muslims had largely dried up. End of article.

From these two examples, it's clear that strength is necessary to avoid the great appeal, attraction, and promise of that false religion, and that false god. It promises peace, but offers only death and disaster; certainly not salvation. Strength is also needed to recognize and defeat that great danger. Those who back away and accept this terror lack that spirit, that Strength to hold fast. They also need the spirit of Wisdom to help make that distinction.

Wisdom

Wisdom is another spirit from God offered to the world, especially the world of believers; those who trust and worship him and his offer of salvation and eternal life. Perhaps the spirit of Wisdom is not only a gift but also a responsibility to use that gift. Perhaps God, in His great wisdom, knows that humans are fundamentally weak - in the light of all things - and must be granted wisdom to understand things that affect each individual as well as all humanity. We must have wisdom to see; and to avoid traps and persuasions.

The call to understand (to have wisdom) begins in the first chapter of Revelation. Verse 3 states, "Blessed is he that readeth, and they that hear the words of this prophecy, and keep those things which are written therein; for the time is at hand." Does this warning not say in simple terms, 'Pay attention to those things happening around you - for they will affect your life?'

In beginning the letters to the seven churches in Chapter 2, Verse 7, John writes from the Words, "He that hath an ear, let him hear what the Spirit saith unto the churches; To him that overcometh will I give to eat of the tree of life, which is in the midst of the paradise of God."

This warning of 'let him hear what the Spirit saith' is repeated several more times in his letters to the churches.

Then, in Chapter 2, Verses 20-22, he writes something that seems very coded until it's associated with another reference in Chapter 17. Verses 20-22 begins, "Notwithstanding I have a few things against thee, because thou sufferest that woman Jezebel, which calleth herself a prophetess, to teach and to seduce my servants to commit fornication, and to eat things sacrificed unto idols. 21) "And I gave her space to repent of her fornications; and she repented not. 22) Behold, I will cast her into a bed, and them that commit adultery with her into great tribulation, except they repent of their deeds."

Although these references are presented early in Revelation in John's letters to the seven churches, that's not necessarily the only target of his writings. That woman 'Jezebel' identified above is the same woman (religion) identified in Chapter 17, which clearly refers to a later time; a time after the seven plagues of the Apocalypse.

Chapter 17 begins, "...Come hither; I will shew unto thee the judgments of the great whore that sitteth upon many waters; 2) With whom the kings of the earth have committed fornication, and the inhabitants of the earth have been made drunk with the wine of her fornication." Verse 5 continues: "And upon her forehead was a name written, MYSTERY BABYLON THE GREAT, THE MOTHER OF HARLOTS AND ABOMINATIONS OF THE EARTH. 6) And I saw the woman drunken with the blood of the saints,...."

Chapter 2, Verse 20 includes the comment, "...and to eat things sacrificed unto idols." Below are two comments that describe an Islamic practice regarding their halal food; first from halalchoices.com:

"Here at Halal Choices we are concerned with the halal slaughter of animals such as beef, lamb and poultry. To be halal certified the animal must be facing Mecca, have its throat cut while still alive and then ritually sacrificed by a Muslim who recites a prayer dedicating the slaughter to Allah. Because the animals must be slaughtered alive, stun guns are often not an option as they can kill an animal before the heart pumps out all the blood." Notice that the animal must be facing Mecca. Might not Mecca, and the process, be considered an 'idol?'

And according to Wikipedia:"Foods that are not halal for Muslims to consume as per various Quranic verses are: pork, blood, intoxicants and alcoholic beverages. Animals killed incorrectly and/or without Allah's name being pronounced before eating. Animals slaughtered in the name of anyone but "Allah". All that has been dedicated or offered in sacrifice to an idolatrous altar or saint or a person considered to be "divine."

Notice the use of the word 'saint.' Now, remember the writing from Chapter 17, Verse 6: "And I saw the woman drunken with the blood of the saints,..." And, could the exclusion of 'a person considered to be "divine" mean none other than God? Could Mecca be one symbol of that idol mentioned in Chapter 2 and Chapter 17?

Furthermore, considering wisdom and the resulting responsibility therefrom, should we not use that wisdom to observe and interpret events surrounding us that support the purposes of that other woman - that harlot. God has given us that wisdom for that purpose. Should we ignore to use it; or should we consider all those events happening around us; events that seem uneventful and unimportant? Or should we question events that are surely associated with the growth and influence of that other 'woman?'

How much respect, awe, and support (sufferest) are we giving the Islamic religion today? Remember John's words in 17:6, ": And when I saw her, I wondered with great admiration." Is that support not growing - rapidly? Consider the following articles that offer answers strongly suggesting our government, pressured by the president, is giving that religion more power and influence:

U.S. Taxpayers Subsidize Overseas Mosques Posted on January 17, 2012 By Gadi Adelman h/t Kasey Jachim:

"With U.S. debt exceeding 15 trillion dollars, what justifies the use of taxpayer dollars to fund rebuilding of mosques overseas?

The story of the U.S. State Department funding mosques overseas was uncovered in July 2010 when reporter Justin Farmer from ABC affiliate WSBTV Channel 2 in Atlanta Georgia did an investigative report. Farmer's story focused on how the U.S. was spending its tax payer dollars while supposedly trying to cut the budget.

I've written on this in the past, but I think it needs a re-visit. I don't think that at a time when our own administration, Congress and Senate have to fight just to come to a 2 month budget agreement we as American taxpayers need to be funding mosques overseas.

What's more, I would bet my Burqa that most Americans have no idea that their hard earned money is going to rebuild mosques.

President Barack Obama announced on January 5, 2012 his administration's new military strategy, saying it will include cutting at least $487 billion in defense spending.

The U.S. budget is so bad that we need to cut $487 billion in defense spending, but Hillary Clinton signed a check for $770 million from the U.S. State Department's USAID program to rebuild Egypt's sewer system. Funny I thought our own infrastructure here in the U.S. is in dire need of repair.

But what was supposed to be a 'sewer' rebuild is much more. The USAID website shows both before and after pictures of one such mosque in Cairo, Egypt. It states:

"The Saleh Talai Mosque in historic Islamic Cairo, dating back to the 10th century, is now active, and open for prayers and tourists. This mosque suffered for decades from rising groundwater contaminated with sewage. USAID, as part of its $770 million Cairo Sewerage Program, allocated $2.3 million for lowering the groundwater at the mosque area, replacing the old sewage collector, and providing a healthier environment for people living in the area."

The Washington times reported on other mosques in August 2010 and emphasized how we are paying for "Muslim triumphalism".

Americans also may be surprised to learn that the United States has been an active participant in mosque construction projects overseas. In April, U.S. Ambassador to Tanzania Alfonso E. Lenhardt helped cut the ribbon at the 12th-century Kizimkazi Mosque, which was refurbished with assistance from the United States under a program to preserve culturally significant buildings. The U.S. government also helped save the Amr Ebn El Aas Mosque in Cairo, which dates back to 642. The mosque's namesake was the Muslim conqueror of Christian Egypt, who built the structure on the site where he had pitched his tent before doing battle with the country's Byzantine rulers. For those who think the Ground Zero Mosque is an example of "Muslim triumphalism" glorifying conquest, the Amr Ebn El Aas Mosque is an example of such a monument – and one paid for with U.S. taxpayer funds.

The same report brought up what can only be called the most important question in this argument. Is it legal for our tax dollars to be used for religious purposes of any kind? The article reported the answer, yet it never received any traction in the media.

But Section 205.1(d) of title 22 of the Code of Federal Regulations prohibits USAID funds from being used for the rehabilitation of structures to the extent that those structures are used for "inherently religious activities." It is impossible to separate religion from a mosque; any such projects will necessarily support Islam.

Well, call me doubtful, but I like to see things for myself so I went and read 205.1(d) of title 22 of the Code of Federal Regulations, it states plainly,

(b) Organizations that receive direct financial assistance from USAID under any USAID program may not engage in inherently religious activities, such as worship, religious instruction, or proselytization, as part of the programs or services directly funded with direct financial assistance from USAID.

One does not have to be an Iranian nuclear scientist to understand the above law. It is illegal, period.

But it doesn't end there; Dr. Laurie Roth wrote in the Canadian Free Press in August 2010,

"What I have uncovered is unacceptable, obscene and should be fought at all levels by the American people. Our State Department is using undisclosed amounts of US tax dollars to build and renovate Islamic Mosques in 27 different countries. They do this under an 'outreach' program with the purpose of fostering 'good will' in Muslim countries. The state department will not reveal just how much they spend on overseas, foreign programs but a very reliable source told me most likely it is in the hundreds of billions."

Oh, so now it's only hundreds of billions, no big deal when we are in debt for trillions.

My own research found more than just 27 countries. According to the Associated Press also August 2010.

This year, the Obama administration will spend nearly $6 million to restore 63 historic and cultural sites, including mosques and minarets, in 55 nations, according to State Department documents.

So now it's 55 countries not 27, but really, what are a few more minarets anyway.

Former Egyptian Muslim and author Nonie Darwish stated during an interview about the U.S. rebuilding mosques, that trying to buy respect in the Middle East only shows our weakness,

"This part of the world has a lot of respect for power and America is not showing its power, it's showing its appeasement. They are laughing all the way to the bank."

"We are rebuilding mosques to support the radicals, not to support the moderates. We are building mosques to issue fatwas of death against people like me."

State Department documents also show that it is providing funding to buy internet computer service for the mosques. Darwish had this to say,

"They call us the Great Satan. So, we're giving them access to really get together against America."

I have written about Obama's Muslim Outreach Program several times dating back to July 2010 but as usual each and every time I point out how much this current administration is trying to buy friendships with those that not only don't like us, but quite frankly would rather see us dead, I get called an Islamaphobe.

The U.S. tax payer dollars continue to flow for projects like this and others. As Jon Christianryter's website reported,

Fifty-five of sixty-three 2010 grants went to Muslim countries. But some of the grants to non-Muslims countries—like China—were nevertheless used to refurbish mosques or other Islamic artifacts.

My question is who oversees this money once the check is written? Do we or for that matter, our State Department really know how it is being spent?

It's bad enough that my tax dollars are going to rebuild mosques and minarets, but I want to know that none of that money is being used to buy weapons that are being used against our men and women in the military." End of article.

Through Jesus, God has granted us the spirit of Wisdom. But, the choice to use that wisdom to search for truth and knowledge is left to each person. As in the overall salvation question, it's a personal choice. One may search for truth to gain wisdom, or one may choose to follow a 'deceiver and blasphemer' without questioning the actions, purposes, or the foundation of that leader.

In Revelation, Jesus cautions many times, "He that hath an ear, let him hear what the Spirit sayeth unto the churches;..." Do not be deceived.

This deceptive power is given to the 'beast' upon his appointment by Satan, described in Chapter 13; Verse 4, "...and they worshipped the beast, saying, Who is like unto the beast? Who is able to make war with him?" Verse 5 continues: "And there was given unto him a mouth speaking great things and blasphemies; ..." Of course, the general description of the beast would include both beasts; the first beast and the false prophet, since the false prophet is described as having the same powers as the first beast.

Finally, the great caution is revealed in Verse 8, "And all that dwell upon the earth shall worship him, whose names are not written in the book of life of the Lamb slain from the foundation of the world."

All believers have been given the spirit of Wisdom to search for the truth. Who will seek those answers to see their names written in the book of life at the end of their time? Who will blindly follow the path of the beast, that antichrist, because they will believe his great words and blasphemies without question? Many who refuse their responsibility that comes with that gift, the spirit of Wisdom, to learn and listen, will blindly continue to follow and not allow their names to be entered into that book.

We must not forget the admonition to use the spirit of Wisdom in identifying the beast named in Revelation. Chapter 13: 18, "Here is wisdom. Let him that hath understanding count the number of the beast; for it is the number of a man; and his number is Six hundred threescore and six."

They will miss the riches that have been promised to them by following the right Word. Those Riches are included within those seven Spirits.

Riches

The concept or idea of Riches being one of the seven Spirits of God is introduced and reinforced in John's letter to the Church at Laodicea. It begins in Chapter 3, Verse 15, "I know they works, that thou art neither cold nor hot; I would thou wert cold or hot." Verse 16, "So then because thou art lukewarm, and neither cold nor hot, I will spew thee out of my mouth."

Verse 17 introduces the concept of riches: "Because thou sayeth, I am rich, and increased with goods, and have need of nothing; and knowest not that thou art wretched, and miserable, and poor, and blind, and naked:" (Laodicea was an economic trade area, where people came to sell and trade their goods. Most were comparatively wealthy based on the wool and textile trade. They were also renowned for preparing and selling special eye salves.)

Verse 18 continues, "I counsel thee to buy of me gold tried in the fire, that thou mayest be rich; and white raiment, that thou mayest be clothed, and that the shame of thy nakedness do not appear; and anoint thine eyes with eyesalve that thou mayest see."

The writing about hot nor cold, white raiment and eye salve have no particular relationship to riches, the riches of the Spirit of the seven Spirits. They are merely conditions associated with the location and economics of Laodicea at that time. They were mentioned earlier in the chapter of the seven Churches. The riches identified in one of the seven Spirits is different.

As introduced above, John was writing about riches given by God, not of earthly things. Chapter 2 also exposes the idea of this different kind of riches. Verse 8, "And unto the angel of the church in Smyrna write; These things saith the first and the last which was dead, and is alive, Verse 9, "I know thy works, and tribulation, and poverty, (but thou art rich) and I know the blasphemy of them which say they are Jews, and are not, but are the synagogue of Satan." For the church at Smyrna, the writing concludes, Verse 10,...""be thou faithful unto death, and I will give thee a crown of life. " Verse 11 repeats the caution: "He that hath an ear, let him hear what the Spirit saith unto the churches..."

Perhaps the clearest meaning of the statement regarding riches is indicated by a verse in Chapter 21. Verse 11 states, "Having the glory of God: and her light was like unto a stone most precious, even like a jasper stone, clear as crystal." The identification of 'her light' is identified in Verse 9 as "...the bride, the Lamb's wife," meaning the church - the religion of Christianity.

Although the subject of Riches might seem somewhat confusing to those who have not used their ears to 'let him hear what the Spirit saith unto the churches;' those who have listened, with intention, understand and feel those riches. Those riches are not those earned by their hands and worldly efforts - they are the riches of the soul and spirit offered by God. Let's consider just a few:

Free Will:

Is not free will a richness? When God put mankind on earth He didn't program them and their descendants to act, think, feel, and respond robotically or without feelings of everything around them. He gave them the ability and the vision to make personal and individual choices.

The first example is the actions of Adam and Eve in the Garden of Eden when they defied God's admonition against eating the forbidden fruit. Convinced by the serpent, Satan, that eating that fruit was normal, they choose to defy the Word of God, The God who made them. God allowed them to make that choice - just as everyone has the ability and the freedom to make that choice today; to accept His Word or not to accept His Word. (Contrary to the religion of that 'strange god' that does not permit free will. That god demands total compliance, or death.)

An Interactive Society:

Just imagine what life would be like if our lives were kept internal, and focused only on food, drink, and shelter; without the ability to interact with other humans - and animals. That interaction, from a stoic viewpoint might be unnecessary for basic survival, but it's certainly necessary to survive as a participant on the earth and in the cosmos. Humans, created by God, must have interaction - one of the great riches granted us to be fully human, and a representation in the Spirit of God. If this were not true - why does man expand space exploration in search of others with whom to interact and to share the

Spirit of God? This is a richness, granted to us, that must be explored and expanded. Likely, that search will continue forever and forever. This suggests another richness; Curiosity.

Curiosity:

Shouldn't we consider curiosity one of the riches granted by God? Just think how boring life would be if we didn't have a curious mind that leads us to new and different things - and different knowledge. Would knowledge ever have any meaning unless led and fed by curiosity? It's like a rope pulling us out of deep water or a deep hole of nothingness. We must be fulfilled; we must find answers to questions and situations to feel more complete and to develop higher regard for ourselves and our fellow humans. Curiosity also leads us to other riches; that of fulfillment.

Fulfillment:

Fulfillment is the result of accomplishing 'rightness.' What would life be if without the opportunity to achieve fulfillment - to accomplish something from one's determined efforts? This is often identified as accomplishing a goal but it's not exactly the same thing.

Accomplishing the goal, if designed for a positive purpose, ordinarily wanes and drifts into the past. It's a point in time that denotes achievement of something seen, imagined, or that has a definite measuring point. The feeling of fulfillment lasts longer. It becomes part of the spirit that allows one to judge his or her feelings of himself or herself against the self-accepted intentions for one's purpose of life.

Perhaps this is the greatest cause for the great failure of our education system today; where a third of our students are not inspired to accomplish the task of learning. They are not instilled with God's

Spirit of Fulfillment. God has been kicked out of our schools; thereby removing that Spirit of Fulfillment so necessary to find one's greatest abilities, accomplishment, and happiness.

Without a purpose, without goals, without fulfillment, life would be for just existing; what would be the purpose for waking up each morning; what would be the purpose of opening one's eyes to look at the new sunrise to plan activities for fulfillment that day and every day? Is it not a richness to have something to accomplish? Ordinarily, that involves the concept of work. The Bible mentions the importance and the responsibility for people to work for their own bread. The concept of work will be discussed in a later section.

Learning:

So - what if we were born with instinctive genes rather than sight, feeling, and curiosity to help us learn? Dogs, cats, and other animals are born with many of those instinctive genes that help them cope with safety and survival; but can they also associate strange new things with familiar and common things that formed the basis of their instincts?

For example, how many animals including cats and dogs do you see killed on roads and highways? Many - and in every location and every environment - are killed every day by not associating the purpose for a roadway or the power of a motorized vehicle. We are given that spirit allowing us to see ahead and behind.

We live every day on learning and understanding; not by instinct. We live this spirit within the great Spirit of Blessings.

Blessings

From the Spirit of God, and through the grace of the Lamb, Jesus, and his sacrifice; Blessings have gone out to all the world to affect and enrich our daily lives. Many of these blessings are acknowledged, almost remotely without deep thought when we 'say the blessing' before each meal, or when we say our nightly prayers. The most common are 'for this food we are about to take' or 'thank you for this day that I have lived.' These are important blessings, but they are by far not the only blessings bestowed upon us. There are many others we take for granted and consider only a part of our daily lives.

Of course, the first blessing is creation itself. God created the universe for his own pleasure and glory. Within that creation, he made the sun and the moon and all the stars. We look up at the sky; in the darkness we see the blessed moon glow and the billions of stars looking back at us. Can you even imagine what the night sky would be like without that blessed gift? It would be only nothingness before your eyes. I can give an example of that feeling from my childhood.

As a child I lived almost two miles from downtown Union, Mississippi, on a dirt road named Gordon Road. The road was named for a man who owned the property my mother bought when I was five years old. It was an unpaved road, part of which went through a swampy area with many overhanging trees. (Now that area has been drained and serves as one of the town's ball parks. It even has one of the Navy's old Blue Angels exhibition planes displayed there.)

When I got older, my younger brother and I often had to walk past that swampy area going to and from town to see a movie, or to attend a normal school event such as a ball game. It was always dark when we walked along the road through the swamp. On those nights when there wasn't moon glow, and when the clouds or haze obscured the stars, we walked through in pitch black.

We progressed largely by memory and the feel of the dirt road, understanding that if we stayed in the deeper ruts we would maintain a straight line. Of course, we made sure we shuffled our steps as loudly as we could so any snakes coiled on the warmer roadway would feel us coming and move into the swamp. I guess it worked because I never felt my feet step on one, and we never got snake bit. However, that wasn't the strangest part.

The strangest part which I remember well was the total feeling of nothingness - detachment from life; from creation and reality. In almost total pitch darkness nothing exists before your eyes. It's as if you were walking in the darkness of space where there is no distance of definition of any object. Thinking back in that darkness it's easy now for me to realize the importance of the moon and the stars. When they are visible, they give definition and distances of things. Things exist and they are seen. It's a blessing to understand that your body, your self-awareness, is positioned in a certain place on this earth; a real blessing.

Even the night time itself is a blessing. Not only does it allow an equalization of temperatures on the face of the earth, it also allows certain other important things to happen. One of the more important things is rest; a time for the body to adjust and repair itself. Again, I digress to my youth for a clear example when I worked in our cotton field; at that time the typical dirt-poor red clay farm you see in very old movie scenes of the 1940s-1950s:

From age twelve to sixteen I worked in the family field and garden. And, since I was the oldest son, having an invalid step-father, I did most of the heavy farm work; which included plowing behind a mule in the four-acre cotton field. In those days if a family had any acreage it was traditional to raise cotton. This was 1950 -1955. Also, at that time and place the school year was only eight months; from September to April. Seriously, this was to allow school-age children in that area to help their families plant crops in the spring-time.

(And, having only an eight-month school year, schools were far more efficient and effective than they are today - even with more time spent in classrooms. In those days, students were taught, and showed great respect and adoration for their teachers. Learning is not about the time spent in the classroom; it's about the purpose and quality of time spent in the classroom. That purpose and quality of time is understood by knowing that learning is one of the blessings of God. If God is not in those classrooms, how can that highest blessing be accepted?)

During the three hottest months it was too dangerous to plow farm animals too long in the sun. Many died from heat stroke if they weren't allowed to rest early afternoon and at night. That blessing was for the work animals as well as for those using those work animals.

Another blessing unknown at that time was boll weevils. Thanks to the boll weevil many small unprofitable farms stopped that unprofitable and difficult tradition. It was a blessing to be relieved from that burdensome and unprofitable task.

Today, as you drive through the state of Mississippi you don't see the small cotton farms that lined the highways and byways before the 1960s. Yes, nighttime is a blessing.

Although some believe the earth and the sun are merely parts of the 'big bang' and evolution, not creation, they were put in their places for a purpose; to be a blessing. The sun is a blessing that allows and creates other blessings. It gives energy for all things on earth - especially for food. Without the sun there would be no food; we would all starve. In our daily prayers we often give thanks for the food we have, but rarely do we ever give thanks for the blessing that allows that food; the sun. (Many ancients did worship a pagan Sun God for that reason.)

And speaking of the sun, it's also a blessing that the sun is the perfect distance from the earth to allow what we have, including food. If the sun were any closer we would all burn. The earth would be parched to a crisp. If the sun were farther away, everything on earth, including us, would freeze. We couldn't live here. Is that not a blessing?

Even the earth, the soil, is a blessing. Without it we would have no place to stand, and a place upon which to build our houses and drive our cars. And along with the earth and soil we have the blessing of discernment. We can move what we want to the soil that allows or supports it, or we can move the soil to another place for a more useful and supportive purpose.

And certainly we can't forget about water. Without water we could not exist, since our physical bodies are mostly water. Without water, if we existed at all, we would be only a few minerals scattered about the earth; perhaps locked inside a rock, or traveling forever in some continuous wind. Yes, one of God's spirits is Blessings. There are Blessings within us and within everything surrounding us. Just being allowed to open our eyes to see those things is, in itself, a blessing.

There are too many to even consider. Perhaps life itself, and its beginning, is the greatest gift - the greatest blessing of all. And considering those things from God we must also consider the spirits of Honor and Glory. They will be considered next.

Honor and Glory

If we trust that the spirits identified above were sent forth into all the world, then we must believe the other two, Honor and Glory, were sent forth into all the world as well. This is that reference again: Revelation 5:6:

"And I beheld, and, lo, in the midst of the throne and of the four beasts, and in the midst of the elders, stood a Lamb as it had been slain, having seven horns and seven eyes, which are the seven Spirits of God sent forth into all the earth." Reference 5:12 listed those seven Spirits:

"Saying with a loud voice, Worthy is the Lamb that was slain to receive power, and riches, and wisdom, and strength, and honor, and glory, and blessings."

How are we mirrors or reflections of that honor and glory? Perhaps 1 Corinthians 3:16-17 gives a clue: 16, "Know ye not that ye are the temple of God, and that the Spirit of God dwelleth in you?" 17, "If any man defile the temple of God, him shall God destroy; for the temple of God is holy, which temple ye are..." If we are "the temple of God" then perhaps God's Spirit is within us. If that Spirit is within us, then we possess through him that honor and glory.

Here is another consideration of that question from Creation.com. The article was written by Russell M. Grigg. It's titled, In The Image of God:

"When God created man in His own image, He purposed that mankind (both man and woman) would resemble God in certain ways, and share certain of the divine prerogatives. Concerning this we note:

1. It was not a physical likeness, but...

Although God is spirit (John 4:24) and does not have a body like a man, when He appeared visibly to men according to the Old Testament record, He did so in the form of a human body (e.g. Genesis 18:1-2; 32:24, 28,30). Dr Henry Morris writes: 'There is something about the human body therefore, which is uniquely appropriate to God's manifestation of Himself, and(since God knows all His works from the beginning of the world—Acts 15:18), He must have designed man's body with this in mind. Accordingly He

63

designed it, not like the animals, but with an erect posture, with an upward gazing countenance, capable of facial expressions corresponding with emotional feelings, and with a brain and tongue capable of articulate, symbolic speech.

Furthermore, the human body was the form in which God the Son would be incarnated or 'made in the likeness of men' (Philippians 2:7). Thus God made man in that bodily form which He Himself would one day assume—the form in which He wished to reveal Himself.

2. It was a mental likeness.

God endowed man with intellectual ability which was and is far superior to that of any animal. Thus man was given a mind capable of hearing and understanding God's communication with him, emotions capable of responding to God in love and devotion, and a will which enabled him to choose whether or not to obey God. Man was thus equipped, not only to 'love God and obey Him for ever', but also to do God's work on earth—to be His regent and govern the creation in co-operation with his Creator. (Author note: recall this when the beast will be defeated; God will not swing the physical sword with His own hands.)

This is seen in God's command to Adam and Eve that they exercise dominion over the earth and its animals (Genesis 1:26,28), in Adam's task of cultivating the garden (Genesis 2:15), and in the statement that Adam gave names to certain of the animals on the earth (Genesis 2:19-20).

Man's intellectual gifts are further seen in his ability to design things and then make them, to appreciate beauty, to compose glorious music, to paint pictures, to write, to count to large numbers and do mathematics, to control and use energy for his own benefit (e.g. fire, electricity, nuclear power), to organize, to reason, to make decisions, to be self-conscious, to laugh at himself, and to think abstractly. All this behaviour is non-instinctive, as distinct from animal behaviour, and as such it is of unlimited variety.

3. It was a moral likeness.

Man only, of all God's creatures, has a spirit or God-consciousness, that is, a capacity for knowing God and holding spiritual communion with Him through prayer, praise, and worship. Since the Fall (Genesis chapter 3), man has had inborn moral awareness of good and evil, or conscience, which he perceives in his spirit.

Man was made not only negatively innocent (that is, without sin), but positively holy, otherwise Adam could not have had communion with God, who cannot look upon iniquity (Habakkuk 1:13). This is further confirmed by Genesis 1:31, when God affirms that everything He had made (including man) was 'very good', which would not have been true if man had been morally imperfect.

4. It was a social likeness.

God's social nature and intrinsic love is seen in the doctrine of the Trinity. God—who is love—created man with a social nature and a need for love. The statement in Genesis 3:8 that 'they heard the voice of the LORD God walking in the garden in the cool of the day' suggests that Adam and Eve enjoyed fellowship and communion with God, perhaps on a daily basis.

God also provided for human fellowship and love in a very special and intimate way. Before He created Eve He said, 'It is not good that the man should be alone; I will make him a help mate for him' (Genesis 2:18). He then made Eve out of a bone taken from Adam (Genesis 2:21-24), a fact which Jesus used in His debate with the

Pharisees to uphold the sanctity of marriage and the intimacy of love within the marriage relationship (Matthew 19:4-6; Mark 10:6-8).

Conclusion

When God created the vegetation and the animals, He made them all 'after its/their kind' (the phrase occurs ten times in Genesis 1:11-25). When He created Adam, He made him after the God-kind — in the image and likeness of God (cf. Acts 17:28). After the Fall, man is still said to be in God's image (Genesis 9:6; 1 Corinthians 11:7) and likeness (James 3:9). However, this image was defiled by man's rebellion at the Fall, and all aspects of God's image were tarnished. Nevertheless, these aspects were perfect in the Lord Jesus Christ, who was and is 'the image of the invisible God' (Colossians 1:15), and 'the express image' of God (Hebrews 1:3), both in His life on earth and in Heaven.

The Apostle Paul says that we are transformed or renewed into the image of God by the Gospel, and that this image is then 'in righteousness and true holiness' (Colossians 3:10; Ephesians 4:24). This is not something that the natural man can bring about by his own efforts, but is the result of our 'receiving Christ' in faith and repentance (John 1:12; Galatians 2:20). It is accomplished by the Holy Spirit (Titus 3:5; Romans 8:28-29), who takes up His abode within God's children (1 Corinthians 3:1; 6:19). 'God is long-suffering towards us, not willing that any should perish, but that all should come to repentance' (2 Peter 3:9).

1 Corinthians 3:7, So then neither is he that planteth any thing, neither he that watereth; but God that giveth the increase. 8, Now he that planteth and he that watereth are one; and every man shall receive his own reward according to his own labour. 9, For we are labourers together with God; ye are God's husbandry, ye are God's building.

Develop to the fullest in service to God and to fellow man. Use those blessings to develop one's abilities and opportunities to the fullest to serve God." End of article.

In summary, perhaps that God Spirit lives within each of us. If that's so, then each of us might receive honor and glory simply by accomplishing those things to better serve His purpose and His designs. And how do we accomplish that task for ourselves by that commandment? The 1Corinthians references gives a definitive clue. We must do something: plant something, build something, make something, accomplish something that will deliver honor and glory to God and that part of ourselves that possesses that honor and glory - in the image of God. Perhaps the short answer is to do something for yourself - in the light of God. Don't be lazy and dependant on others to take care of you. Plant something; and God will help you water it.

Even with our best intentions, however, and even with our purest effort to follow the Words of God; that dragon, that serpent who tempted Eve in the Garden of Eden is ever present near us to continue that temptation to avoid God's will. That will be the topic of the next chapters; the battle between good and evil. And, there are two participants: Christianity and Islam.

The whole of the Book of Revelation is to identify the Beast that will attack Christianity and the whole world. It describes the rise of Islam, the horror and evil it creates and permeates; and how God's Spirit will eventually defeat it. It reveals that Islam is guided by that same serpent, Satan, who influenced Adam and Eve in the Garden of Eden. Christianity will be reviewed first.

Chapter 3
Lamb and Beast

Christianity

The identity and description of the first woman, Christianity, begins with the first verse in Chapter 12 of Revelation. "And there appeared a great wonder in heaven, a woman clothed with the sun, and the moon under her feet, and upon her head a crown of twelve stars;" The word 'great' throughout Revelation references one from God, or Christ; such as a great star. The 'twelve stars' is a major clue, since it likely refers to the twelve Jewish tribes. However, since most Jews rejected the idea of Jesus as the Messiah, it's also possible that these twelve stars represented the twelve apostles after Jesus was born. The connotation in this verse is that the twelve stars were upon the religion not upon the person. 'Clothed with the sun' certainly would indicate greatness and light. The word 'moon' might suggest humility and worldliness.

Verse 2 continues: "And she being with child cried, travailing in birth, and pained to be delivered.." The Messiah was expected even before Jesus was born. During that early time, Rome and the puppet leaders such as King Herod were wary of anyone rising up from the Jewish community to challenge them. Jews were totally subdued - pained. Herod's actions were guided by that old serpent, Satan.

Verse 3 introduces another great red star, "And there appeared another wonder in heaven; and behold a great red dragon, having seven heads and ten horns, and seven crowns upon his heads." Of course, the red dragon, or any great dragon, mentioned in the Bible identifies Satan, the Devil. He thought he should be God, and tried to replace Him. This will be explained later.

This entry suggests Satan was in heaven with those who supported him. Verse 9 says they were cast out to deceive the whole world. This was after that Satan's battle in heaven with Michael and his angels. Verse 4 says "...and the dragon stood before the woman which was ready to be delivered, for to devour her child as soon as it was born." But, what of the seven heads and ten horns?

Many interpret this as the seven hills of Rome, and Roman leaders of the past - up until the time John wrote Revelation. They suggest the great Roman Empire will be revitalized. This interpretation seems to have no relevance, since it implies that Rome would be a major player during the time of the great tribulation, which didn't happen at the time Rome held great power. Although this mention of the seven heads is included in this reference, perhaps it's meant for another time.

A clearer and more timely mention of the seven heads and their rise from the sea is detailed in the first verse of the next chapter, 13, which says, "And I stood upon the sand of the sea, and saw a beast rise up out of the sea, having seven heads and ten horns, and upon his horns ten crowns, and upon his heads, the name of blasphemy." What does this mean, other than the rise of the antichrist - Muhammad? Muhammad as the antichrist will be discussed later.

Ordinarily, the mention of the sea in Revelation refers to the sea of humanity, people. In this verse, however, the word sand is added to the description; which might suggest a real sea of water. Most likely, those seven heads rising out of the sea represent our seven continents, onto which Islam has spread. The ten horns are the ten major nations of Islam wearing those ten crowns.

The meaning of these two verses couldn't be more clear. Satan, in the form of Rome and King Herod, tried to destroy that new religion before it came into existence. When Herod heard a new 'king of the Jews was to be born' he had all the young males from new borns to two-year olds slaughtered. This action is identified in history as the 'Massacre of the Innocents' or the 'Slaughter of the Innocents.'

Verse 5 clearly identifies this new born as Christ, "And she (the woman, Christianity) brought forth a man child, who was to rule all nations with a rod of iron: and her child was caught up unto God, and to his throne." The next verse, 6, begins a date with a time link that sets the stage to understand the two women and the ultimate war against good and evil; against Christianity and Islam. It states:

"And the woman fled into the wilderness, where she hath a place prepared of God, that they should feed her there a thousand two hundred and threescore days." The time given is presented as three and a half years; however that's a code for three hundred and fifty years. That connection will be made shortly in the next verses.

The next few verses, 7-13, describe the battle in heaven between Satan and Michael and their angels. In concludes in Verse 13, "And when the dragon saw that he was cast unto the earth, he persecuted the woman which brought forth the man child." This describes the time when Christ, along with many of his apostles and followers were persecuted, crucified, and beheaded. This continued during that next three hundred and fifty years mentioned earlier. Then, an amazing thing happened that confirmed the time line. Christianity suddenly had a protector. Verse 14 describes that shift:

"And to the woman were given two wings of a great eagle, that she might fly into the wilderness, into her place, where she is nourished for a time, and times, and half a time, from the face of the serpent."

This provides the time line and the information, the key that unlocks the codes to most of the information presented in Revelation. That information is provided by 'three hundred and fifty years' and 'time, times, and half a time.' This last time also equals three hundred and fifty years. Now, let's consider what happened at the end of each three hundred and fifty years after Christ was crucified.

At the end of the first three hundred and fifty years, Christianity was protected by Rome. The symbol for Rome was 'two wings of a great eagle.' It was the standard that was carried before troops marching into battle. So, how did this happen? An excellent answer is given by Richard Cavandish at Historytoday.com. This is that article:

"Roman politics after the Emperor Diocletian abdicated in AD 305 was confusingly complicated as emperors and deputy emperors of the West and of the East contended for power. Among them was Flavius Valerius Constantinus, known to history as Constantine the Great. Acclaimed as emperor by his troops in York in AD 306, he was appointed Caesar or deputy emperor of the West by Diocletian's successor, Galerius. Constantine was in charge of Britain and Gaul, but his brother-in-law Maxentius waged war against Galerius and seized Italy and Rome itself.

Galerius died in ad 311 and early the next year Constantine invaded Italy, won battles at Turin and Verona and marched on Rome. Maxentius came out to fight and was destroyed at the Milvian Bridge, which carried the Via Flaminia over the Tiber into the city. The battle was one of a succession of victories that in AD 324 made Constantine master of the entire Roman Empire, but it is most famous for its link with his conversion to Christianity, which would prove to be one of the most important events in world history.

The story, or a story, of what happened was told by Eusebius of Caesarea, a Christian biblical scholar and historian who wrote the first biography of Constantine soon after the emperor's death. He knew Constantine well and said he had the story from the emperor himself. Constantine was a pagan monotheist, a devotee of the sun god Sol Invictus, the unconquered sun. However before the Milvian Bridge battle he and his army saw a cross of light in the sky above the sun with words in Greek that are generally translated into Latin as In hoc signo vinces ('In this sign conquer'). That night Constantine had a dream in which Christ told him he should use the sign of the cross against his enemies. He was so impressed that he had the Christian symbol marked on his soldiers' shields and when the Milvian Bridge battle gave him an overwhelming victory he attributed it to the god of the Christians.

This story was generally accepted for centuries, but today's historians who are not believers in prophetic visions and dreams have serious doubts about it. The earliest account of the battle, dating from AD 313, mentions nothing about a vision or a dream. It says that Maxentius drew up his army on the bank of the Tiber. He had cut the bridge itself, but in case of defeat he could retreat to Rome across a temporary bridge made of boats. When Constantine's cavalry charged, however, Maxentius's men were driven in flight across the bridge of boats, which collapsed under them, and many were drowned, including Maxentius himself. His head was cut off and carried into the city on a spear by the triumphant Constantine and his men.

According to another early account, written within two years of the battle by the Christian author Lactantius, who had been at Constantine's court for some time, the emperor had a dream in which he was told to mark 'the heavenly sign of God' on his soldiers' shields. He did as instructed, had the sign, whatever exactly it was, inscribed on the shields and attributed his victory against odds to the god of the Christians. In AD 315 the Senate dedicated a triumphal arch in Rome to Constantine (it may have been built originally for Maxentius), with an inscription praising him because 'with divine instigation' he and his army had won the victory. It tactfully refrained from saying which god had provided the 'instigation' and citizens could credit it to Sol Invictus or the Christian deity or whichever god they chose.

What is not in doubt is that Constantine became a believing Christian who vigorously promoted Christianity without trying to force it down pagan throats. Diocletian and Galerius had persecuted the Christians savagely, but in AD 311 Galerius had granted them freedom of worship. In AD 313 Constantine's Edict of Milan proclaimed that 'no one whatsoever should be denied the opportunity to give his heart to the observance of the Christian religion.' He appointed Christians to high office and gave Christian priests the same privileges as pagan ones. He taught his soldiers to respect Sunday, the day of the sun, which was also the Christian sabbath.

By AD 323 the birthday of Sol Invictus on December 25th had become the birthday of Christ. The emperor strove to iron out theological disagreements among Christians and in AD 325 he personally attended the Council of Nicaea, which formulated the doctrine of the Trinity. He also built magnificent churches, including Santa Sophia in his capital city of Byzantium, renamed Constantinople. When he died in AD 337 Christianity was well on its way to becoming the state religion of the Roman Empire and Constantine considered himself the 13th apostle of Jesus Christ. Constantine's actions and conversion resulted in formation of the Roman Catholic Church." End of Article.

Now, let's add the times: the first time of persecution was three hundred and fifty years, plus the second time of protection was another three hundred and fifty years. That puts the next significant time at seven hundred AD. What happened then?

Verses 15 and 16 repeated the fact that the woman had been persecuted by the serpent, but the earth opened up her mouth and swallowed the flood the serpent had sent out to destroy that woman -

Christianity. Verse 17 describes what happened at the end of that seven hundred years:

"And the dragon was wroth with the woman, and went to make war with the remnant of her seed, which keep the commandments of God, and have the testimony of Jesus Christ." But, where did this new threat come from? That will be answered in the next chapter titled: The Beast Rises. Before we go there, however, let's identify and describe the other woman in Revelation; Islam. That description begins in Chapter 6, then goes into full detail in Chapter 17.

Islam

Certainly, you've heard of the four horses of the Apocalypse. These are identified in Revelation, Chapter 6. These horses appeared as the first four seals were opened. The first horse was the white horse, which represented Christ and his conquering forces. The next horse introduced was the red horse. This was the first clue in the Bible of the coming beast of Islam. After the second seal was opened in Verse 3, Verse 4 continues:

"And there went out another horse that was red: and power was given to him that sat thereon to take peace from the earth, and that they should kill one another: and there was given unto him a great sword."

This one small and simple verse gives the full story and description of Islam. Islam has two heads, and those two heads are killing one another - as they are in the Muslim nations today. Islam also has a great sword, many followers, and they are taking peace from the earth. They have done this since they (Islam) were created about 700 AD. They are taking peace from all over the world today.

They claim to be a religion of peace; perhaps that should be stated as the religion that destroys peace. That's exactly what this verse says.

75

Chapter 13 describes the rise of the beast and the false prophet, but we will discuss that detail later. Now, let's return to understanding this other woman; Islam. That greater detail is presented in Chapter 17, after another introduction in Chapter 16.

Chapter 16 begins by introducing the seven angels and their seven vials of wrath: "And I heard a great voice out of the temple saying to the seven angels, Go your ways, and pour out the vials of the wrath of God upon the earth." The remainder of Chapter 16 explains what happened when the seven vials were poured upon the earth. Chapter 17 begins when one of those seven angels tells John to come and see what happened:

"And there came one of the seven angels which had the seven vials, and talked with me, saying unto me, Come hither; I will shew unto thee the judgment of the great whore that sitteth upon many waters: 2) With whom the kings of the earth have committed fornication, and the inhabitants of the earth have been made drunk with the wine of her fornication. 3) So he carried me away in the spirit into the wilderness; and I saw a woman sit upon a scarlet colored beast, full of names of blasphemy, having seven heads and ten horns." Now, this next part becomes very coded. Remember, this woman sits upon a scarlet colored beast; the same as the red horse described above.

Verse 4 adds another color: "And the woman was arrayed in purple and scarlet color, and decked with gold and precious stones and pearls, having a golden cup in her hand full of abominations and filthiness of her fornication." Here, we must pause to understand the relevance of these few words. This seems very coded and complicated until we consider each word.

We know this woman, Islam, was riding a red horse; which is the same as the scarlet colored beast. But, what about purple? This color came out of nowhere; or did it? This woman was arrayed in oil, which gave her great wealth, gold and precious stones, but that golden cup allowed Islam the power to be unchallenged for their fornication and abominations - especially against young boys and girls. Can you just imagine the horror of a young girl, before the age of ten, being raped by an older man - or any man; and that so-called religion accepts this as normal. Is there any greater fornication than this? This is only one of the acts of that religion's acceptable fornication and abomination. But what about their power base of oil; purple and scarlet?

Research shows that the base color of these two colors: red (scarlet) and purple, is amber. Amber is the base color of oil. Essentially, these statements say that these fornicators are wealthy because of their oil. And that wealth and power gives them the freedom to do what they choose without being challenged by rational humanity. They wield that power against anyone who would dare question them and their 'religious' activities. This is Islam. And how can we be sure this is Islam. The next two verses make it very clear:

Verse 5 identifies that woman sitting upon that scarlet colored beast, "And upon her forehead was a name written, MYSTERY BABYLON THE GREAT, THE MOTHER OF HARLOTS AND ABOMINATIONS OF THE EARTH." (These capital letters were included in this verse.) This also describes the rider of the red horse; the mother and her harlots. Then Verse 6 tells exactly who they are:

"And I saw the woman drunken with the blood of the saints and with the blood of the martyrs of Jesus; and when I saw her, I wondered with great admiration." Islam is the only religion that has been and is 'drunken with the blood' of Christians. This is the clearest definition of Islam in the Bible. John's admiration puzzled the angel and the angel responded in the next verse:

"And the angel said unto me, Wherefore didst thou marvel? I will tell thee the mystery of the woman, and of the beast that carrieth her, which hath the seven heads and ten horns." The angel continued the description of that woman and that beast to the end of the chapter.

However, the next four verses, 8-11, are very coded and haven't definitely been interpreted by anyone, although there are a few guesses out there by scholars. The mystery begins with Verse 8:

"The beast that thou sawest was, and is not; and shall ascend out of the bottomless pit, and go into perdition: and they that dwell on the earth shall wonder, whose names were not written in the book of life from the foundation of the world, when they behold the beast that was, and is not, and yet is." Let's examine one possible consideration. This could be a metaphor from an event that happened to Muhammad. 'He was; they thought he was dead; and he rose again to lead them - referring to his Muslim followers.'

This symbolic even occurred during the Battle of Uhud in 625 AD between Muhammad and his Muslim forces from Medina and a Meccan army. During that battle, Muhammad was struck in the face by three arrows from the Meccans. Also three of his front teeth were knocked out from thrown rocks. When he fell as if dead, his Muslim army retreated to a nearby hill. When he suddenly rose to accompany his men, it was considered a miracle which some considered a resurrection. With this metaphor in mind, let's continue with the next three puzzling verses beginning with Verse 9:

"And here is the mind which hath wisdom. The seven heads are seven mountains, on which the woman sitteth." (As stated earlier, this probably represents the seven continents rising from the sea. This is also stated in the first verse of Chapter 13.) 10) And there are seven kings: five are fallen, and one is, and the other is not yet come; and when he cometh, he must continue a short space. 11) And the beast that was, and is not, even he is the eighth, and is of the seven, and goeth into perdition."

Since this was written during the beginning of Christianity, some interpreters believe the 'five that are fallen' refers to major dynasties prior to the rise of Christianity, such as Greek, Roman, Hittite,

Egyptian, etc. Then we move into Papal rule then finally Ottoman Islam. That metaphor from Muhammad might suggest that one great national leader who exists today might lose that power for awhile and then rise to an even greater power that might cause much perdition - destruction. This destruction might be caused by the consolidation of power by one leader, as suggested in Verse 12:

"And the ten horns which thou sawest are ten kings, which have received no kingdom as yet; but receive power as kings one hour with the beast. 13) These have one mind, and shall give their power and strength unto the beast." First, we must consider that time of 'one hour.' As in other cases, for example the three and a half years for three hundred and fifty years; that time could mean some other time. It would be reasonable to think one year instead of one hour. It would take more than one hour to consolidate power with ten kings- nations. And, their leader would have been a leader who would have disappeared from that leadership, then would appear again as a leader of the ten: 'was, was not. then is.' Now, merely as an illustration, let's consider an example:

Currently, Barack Obama is president of the United States: the comparable position of a 'king.' Unless he does something to prevent it, he will leave that kingly office in the near future. He will no longer be there; he will be 'was not.' Now, just imagine that sometime in the near future the Islamic nation becomes so strong, or as an act of appeasement to 'peaceful' bloodthirsty Muslims; Barack Obama is elected to another high position; such as head of the United Nations. He would be 'then is.' For a 'king' who has shown such love and favoritism to Islam, would this not be a dangerous situation for the rest of the peaceful world, especially after a year to consolidate all that power spread over the seven continents? The question would then be; what course of action would he promote? Of course, this is just an example. The next verse, 14, explains the result:

"These shall make war with the Lamb, and the Lamb shall overcome them; for he is Lord of lords and King of kings: and they that are with him are called, and chosen, and faithful. 15) And he (that angel continuing his explanation) saith unto me The waters which thou sawest, where the whore sitteth, are peoples, and multitudes, and nations, and tongues."

Verse 16 explains how the rider of the red horse (6:4) shall kill one another. "And the ten horns which thou sawest upon the beast (mother Islam); these shall hate the whore (her harlot,) and shall make her desolate and naked, and shall eat her flesh, and burn her with fire. 17) For God hath put in their hearts to fulfill his will, and to agree, and give their kingdom unto the beast, until the words of God shall be fulfilled. 18) And the woman which thou sawest is that great city (Babylon-Islam) which reigneth over the kings of the earth."

Chapter 18 gives the results of that fulfillment, but only the first two verses will be included here to show those results. The remainder of Chapter 18 will be discussed in a later chapter.

"And after these things I saw another angel come down from heaven, having great power and the earth was lightened with his glory. 2) And he cried mightily with a strong voice, saying, Babylon the great is fallen, is fallen, and is become the habitation of devils, and the hold of every foul spirit, and a cage of every unclean and hateful bird."

Now, let's turn to the rise of that beast having seven heads and ten horns. That description is given in Chapter 13. Chapter 13 also includes the information about the 'mark of the beast' which is the concept most people think of when they hear mention of Revelation.

Chapter 4
The Beast Rises

C hapter 13 describes the rise of the beast, commonly identified as the antichrist and the second beast, also identified as the false prophet. Before we begin that analysis however, let's review the last verse in Chapter 12, which explains Satan's plan for those two antichrists. Verse 17 reads:

"And the dragon was wroth with the woman, and went to make war with the remnant of her seed, which keep the commandments of God, and have the testimony of Jesus Christ." This says the devil failed in his attempt to kill the woman, Christianity, when it was first born, so he planned a new strategy - the creation of the other woman, Islam, to destroy Christianity. The first verse of Chapter 13 begins that explanation:

"And I stood upon the sand of the sea, and saw a beast rise up out of the sea, having seven heads and ten horns, and upon his horns ten crowns, and upon his heads the name of blasphemy." This short verse contains many concepts, so let's try to understand them.

As revealed earlier in this writing, the mention of a sea refers to the sea of humanity, people, not to an actual body of water. In this case the beast rose up from people of the earth, not from a godly spirit in heaven. And, we have already considered the seven heads as continents; and the ten horns as leaders, specifically leaders of nations. "...and upon his heads the name of blasphemy" refers back to the letters to the seven churches; specifically 2:9, which states, "...and I know the blasphemy of them which say they are Jews, and are not, but are the synagogue of Satan." The blasphemy is that of someone, in this case Muhammad, claiming to be on a higher order than Jesus Christ. To claim to replace Christ or God is the highest order of blasphemy; that's exactly what Muhammad and the whole body of Islam has done. The seven heads and ten horns have already been discussed in the last chapter. Now, let's consider Verse 2:

"And the beast which I saw was like unto a leopard, and his feet were as the feet of a bear, and his mouth as the mouth of a lion: and the dragon gave him his power, and his seat, and great authority."

Although this might suggest the power of a large and powerful individual person, the word beast also suggests the scarlet colored beast ridden by the that woman - Islam. The word beast in this case likely represents Islam. Now let's consider these three descriptive animals from that perspective:

Perhaps the leopard represents stealth and deceit; as Islam claims to be descended from Abraham and Ishmael to hide their moon god origin. Also, we have the Muslim Brotherhood slithering and sliding into corners of our leadership and culture to eventually eliminate who we are; like a leopard that gets into position and then suddenly pounces upon its unsuspecting victim. Yes, the Muslim Brotherhood has a written plan to do just that; it's called the Memorandum, and the process of 'Settlement.' This plan will be discussed later.

The bear could represent power and force. Bears are very strong animals and can become intimidating when approaching an unarmed person - even if the person is lightly armed. Should Islam be considered strong? Their strength is even revealed in 6:4, which has been discussed earlier: "And there went out another horse that was red: and power was given to him that sat thereon to take peace from the earth, and that they should kill one another; and there was given unto him a great sword." Yes, they have power.

And, what is a lion noted for? His great roar from his mouth. The beast is recognized throughout the Bible for his strong words and blasphemies. Even Verse 5 in this Chapter reads, "And there was given unto him a mouth speaking great things and blasphemies; and power was given unto him to continue forty and two months." Now, what does the forty two months, three and a half years, represent? Although there's no direct connection, one might only guess that's the time associated with the time of great tribulation. That's briefly stated in Daniel. It concerns the agreement, that covenant of seven nations.

Daniel 9:26 says, in part, "...and the end thereof shall be with a flood, and unto the end of the war desolations are determined." Next, Verse 27 continues, "And he shall confirm the covenant with many for one week; (seven years) and in the midst of the week he shall cause the sacrifice and the oblation to cease, and for the overspreading of abominations he shall make it desolate, even until the consummation, and that determined shall be poured upon the desolate." That 'in the midst' will be a time of three and a half years. In summary, The covenant will be for seven years, and after half that time, the beast will void that covenant and will begin an atrocity. That atrocity will cause tribulation throughout the world.

Now, let's return to the rising of the beast, Islam, in Chapter 13. Verse 3 mentions that deadly wound again; likely this is the one suffered by Muhammad at the Battle of Uhud, when he was thought to be killed by arrows and stones. "And I saw one of his heads as it were wounded to death; and his deadly wound was healed; and all the world wondered after the beast." Another interpretation some make of this verse is that one country was thought to be annihilated, but recovered itself to be an effective part of Islam again. For example, could what's happening now in Syria fulfill this event?

The next three verses, 6-8, explain his power and actions while he exists on earth. This is likely a short version of Muhammad's life. "And he opened his mouth in blasphemy against God (which Muhammad did) to blaspheme his name, and his tabernacle, and them that dwell in heaven. And it was given unto him to make war with the saints, and to overcome them; and power was given him over all kindreds, and tongues, and nations. And all that dwell upon the earth shall worship him, whose names are not written in the book of life of the Lamb slain from the foundation of the world."

These things happened during Muhammad's lifetime. This leader of the 'peaceful' religion killed everyone who refused to worship him as the only true prophet. His followers are still doing that today, all over the world. That 'peace' is killing thousands of people of all kindreds, and tongues, and nations. They continue to follow the design of Satan; to take peace from the earth. But, historically speaking, Muhammad's personal reign didn't last that long; only with one man's lifetime. Two seemingly out of place verses become very important in understanding Islamic history. They show the transition; Verses 9 and 10:

"If any man have an ear, let him hear. He that leadeth into captivity shall go into captivity: he that killeth with the sword must be killed with the sword. Here is the patience and the faith of the saints."

Why are these two verses important? Because they show the end of Muhammad. Verse 9 says to 'pay attention' to what's to come. Verse 10 said those who kill violently will die violently, although Muhammad was not killed with a sword. He died from poison food prepared by one of his wives; a conquered woman who had been the wife and brother of two of his victims. In another reference it's said he was killed 'without hand.' The verse doesn't say that was the end of Muhammad, but the next two verses,11-12, give that extra clue:

"And I beheld another beast coming up out of the earth; and he had two horns like a lamb, and he spake like a dragon.12) And he exerciseth all the power of the first beast before him, and causeth the earth and them which dwell therein to worship the first beast, whose deadly wound was healed."

Now, this new information holds great significance. First, it asks the reader to pay attention; which means something important is about to be revealed. Then it reveals two pieces of great information. First, it reveals that the beast who rose from the sea with an injured head, and thought dead, was a person not a country. It was Muhammad, whose deadly wound was healed on the battlefield at Uhud. Second, it reveals that his successor, the second beast, will appear to be a peace maker; he will have two small horns like a lamb. Then it suggests his words spoken in peace will actually be words to represent the dragon - Satan.

What does the phrase, 'And he exerciseth all the power of the first beast before him' mean? It means he will be the leader of a nation and a great army; just like Muhammad was. Muhammad was the leader of the 'Islamic Nation' and he led a powerful and deadly armed force. This second beast, this false prophet, has great power and he pretends to be a peace maker. So, are there any clues to suggest who this supporter of that first beast, Muhammad, might be? Let's explore further in the next verse, 13:

"And he doeth great wonders, so that he maketh fire come down from heaven on the earth in the sight of men."

When John wrote this, he didn't write from an explanation from Christ; he wrote from his vision of what Christ presented to him. At that time, there were no airplanes, no tanks, no artillery; not even a simple little BB gun. John saw fire coming down from the sky so that's how he wrote it. And, until the last century of so, any fire coming down from the sky would have been considered a miracle. Today, it's not a miracle because we know planes and drones shoot fire from the sky as a routine practice. It's no longer a miracle. In his vision, John would have considered it a miracle; as he wrote it. But, we must consider another possible deception from that modern fire from the sky.

Of course, a modern leader would not drop fire; bombs, rockets, or bullets from the sky just to display a miracle to persuade someone to believe him or her. Ordinarily, if not always, those weapons are dropped from the sky to kill someone, or to persuade a force to yield to a higher military force. So, let's consider another possible use of using that firepower as a deception to others. Verse 14 suggests a hidden clue that offers that possibility. This continues from Verse 13 above:

"And deceiveth them that dwell on the earth by the means of those miracles which he had power to do in the sight of the beast; saying to them that dwell on the earth, that they should make an image to the beast, which had the wound by the sword, and did live." Now, consider another possibility offered by this verse. Remember, the point here for that fire from the sky is deception; the verse does not say 'to defeat.' So, let's use another modern day example.

This chapter clearly describes the actions by the beast and by the second beast, that false prophet. The beast is gone; we are now dealing with the false prophet. He is a 'false' one. So, for example; what if a leader, that false prophet, were to be in a position that required him to wage war against those fervent followers of the beast to protect those who had promoted him to that prominent position based on deception; that he would protect them? To understand this we must first remember and combine the two terms; deception and false prophet. His goal would be to deceive, to gain more power so his power might one day be unchallenged; such as in a condition of martial law.

If that were the case, then the false prophet would control and limit the amount of 'miracle fire from heaven' to present a false show of force against the beast, but really had no intentions of defeating that beast he so worshiped. In this case he would appear to 'do great wonders' by presenting that false and deceitful image. By his actions he would be protecting and preserving the power of his origin, that first beast. Just as an example; could this be considered the action by Barack Obama in his fight against radical Islamic terrorists today? Oh, wait, he 'never will be at war against radical Islamic terrorists' so he would never drop bombs as a deception to pretend to defeat them - would he?

That other part of Verse 14, "...saying to them that dwell on the earth, that they should make an image to the beast, which had the wound by the sword, and did live," is more difficult to understand - at this current time. Conditions haven't arrived to even consider this as a possibility. So, at this time there seems to be two considerations. First, is the short-term possibility of an image of the beast. This considers that concept that the word 'beast' describes Muhammad, the false prophet, and the religion itself.

There's a powerful movement today, in the Middle East and Africa to form what's called a caliphate. So, what is a caliphate? According to thewire.com:

"A caliphate is an Islamic state. It's led by a caliph, who is a political and religious leader who is a successor (caliph) to the Islamic prophet Muhammad. His power and authority is absolute." (Is this not an image to the beast, which had the wound by the sword and did live?)

And we should consider another definition of a caliphate from Wikipedia:

"A caliphate is a form of Islamic government led by a caliph, a person considered a political and religious successor to the Islamic prophet, Muhammad, and a leader of the entire Muslim community. The Rashidun caliphs, who directly succeeded Muhammad as leaders of the Muslim community, were chosen through shura, a process of community consultation that some consider an early form of Islamic democracy. During the history of Islam after the Rashidun period, many Muslim states, almost all of them hereditary monarchies, have claimed to be caliphates. Even though caliphates were thought to go back to Muhammad, they were not thought of as having the same prophetic power as he did.

The Sunni branch of Islam stipulates that, as a head of state, a caliph should be elected by Muslims or their representatives (in practice, however, this devolved into a hereditary monarchic system soon after the beginning of Islam) and from Quraysh. Followers of Shia Islam, however, believe a caliph should be an Imam chosen by God from the Ahl al-Bayt (the "Family of the House", Muhammad's direct descendants).

Abu Bakr al-Baghdadi's group the Islamic State of Iraq and the Levant (ISIL) declared its governmental structure a 'caliphate' on June 29, 2014 after taking control of large swathes of territory in Syria (which for a prolonged period of time comprised over 50% of that country, and Iraq. Nevertheless, it is regarded by much of the Muslim world and Muslim scholars to be an illegitimate caliphate within the basis of Islam.)"

A major question at this time, if this is the case; if formation of a caliphate represents that image of the beast, then is that representation of the caliphate itself or someone leading that caliphate? It would seem from the writing that the image would be of the person; however, that false religion doesn't allow images to be made of the beast, that antichrist Muhammad. That, then, would strongly suggest the image would be made in the image of the religion - the caliphate itself. And, there's another key word in that verse: it says an image 'to' the beast not an image 'of' the beast. Again, this would suggest the image would be of the original religion - that bloodthirsty reign of Muhammad. Then the next verse,15, switches words from 'to' to 'of.'

"And he had power to give life unto the image of the beast, that the image of the beast should both speak, and cause that as many as would not worship the image of the beast should be killed."

Now, we citizens of the United States read this verse and the next two and imagine this affects us as we sit in the comfort and safety of our homes. Since it's the Bible, and we are a Christian nation (except in Obama's thinking - and words) we feel that if we don't convert to Islam, and pray to that false god, that we will be killed. It's possible that could happen to some, or many, but in most likelihood it refers to those living in and under the control of those beastly monsters, such as the new caliphate and others who represent those same ungodly principles.

On the other hand, non-Muslims are also being slaughtered in other regions and countries controlled by Muslims. To fulfill the word of their religion, they must not tolerate others; otherwise they will not go to heaven to claim their 72 virgins and macho studs loaded with Viagra. (Why does that so-called religion have such a fascination for sex? Did Muhammad set that example by accumulating many wives during his heinous conquests? Instead, shouldn't they be focused on love and salvation?)

For those being slaughtered for not being a Muslim, no matter where they are, the Apocalypse is already happening to them. They are already living those days described in Revelation; it's not something to come in the future. That future is already here. Perhaps understanding this helps give answers to the remaining verses in Chapter 13:

Verse16: "And he (the second beast - the false prophet) causeth all, both small and great, rich and poor, free and bond, to receive a mark in their right hands, or in their foreheads; 17) And that no man might buy or sell, save he that had the mark, or the name of the beast, or the number of his name." Now, here is the really strange part; the first verse in the next chapter, 14, explains what this means; and it's one of the references of Christ. It says:

"And I looked, and lo, a Lamb stood on the mount Sion, and with him an hundred forty and four thousand, having his Father's name written in their foreheads."

This likely refers to the 144,000 Jews that would be converted to Christians before the end times. At this time, God's name is written in their foreheads. Now, would this not suggest that they have merely accepted God into their minds, their foreheads, and there's not a big placard on their foreheads that says 'God?' The same would be true for the beast's name. This mark is only a metaphor for a sign of acceptance. Identification of a mark in the right hand offers other possibilities. Could it be a knife, a firearm, a card that identifies them as Muslim, or even the Islamic flag one might hold. Whatever it is, it will become clear in the near future. Before we review the last verse in this chapter, let's first present a possible alternative to that mark in the right hand.

There's a strong movement toward what's considered a one-world order. If that were to happen, if there were to be a one-world government in the near future, that would present another option for that mark. And, since there's much fear and apprehension about protecting world citizens against uncertainty and terrorists, that movement to consolidate policing and security might become too strong to resist.

The world, or many countries might come together to form a consortium. Or, even that caliphate itself and with other Muslim nations might form their own combined protectorate. Another consideration; that might be the ulterior motive for the great world-wide movement to control 'climate change.' That movement is being controlled by the same leadership that also proposes 'sustainable development;' that new catch word for 'Agenda 21.' Satan is at work everywhere to replace God; and under many names.

In either case, if this were to occur, what would then happen? Certainly to maintain control and security every person must be instantly identifiable. One way could be something in the form of a passport for every citizen under that jurisdiction. That piece of paper in the right hand would be a 'mark.' But, there's also a more insidious possibility - that infamous computer chip actually placed in the right hand; in the thick part between the thumb and the index finger.

This chip could be used not only for identification, but also for purchasing and selling. Each person could be recognized from an identification code of eighteen numbers from some distance away; for example from wireless readers on storefronts along a sidewalk, or even at greater distances; maybe even from airplanes or drones flying overhead. Imagine the fear and despair. Now, let's review that last verse in Chapter 18; that infamous 666 number.

"Here is wisdom. Let him that hath understanding count the number of the beast: for it is the number of a man; and his number is Six hundred threescore and six." That's a total of 666. People throughout history have tried to find a name in this total by considering letters and numbers in the Greek alphabet, counting the numbers of dynasties and other complicated methods and formats. Some have even tried to suggest this is in some way a representation of Nero, and even the Pope, within certain manifestations of some complicated format. First, they have assumed this was the number of the antichirst, the first beast. It's not; it's the number of the second beast, that false prophet.

So, at this point I must ask a simple question. Would Christ, who was trying to warn us about a great danger from a certain person actually code that name in such a way that it would be impossible to determine? I think not; I believe he made it simple so we would understand. Otherwise, what's the purpose for including that information? And, that simplicity is too simple. It says to 'count the number of the beast; for it is the number of a man.' It says to 'count.' So, 6+6+6 equals18. That's counting. In a simple manner that would suggest the name would consist of 18 letters. Now, let's consider a random name just as an example. Let's try:

BARACKHUSSEINOBAMA

and see if that fits. Interesting; just a random name fits as an example. Now, one might also ask if that number 18 might have any validity to support that code. Yes; there's a check word, a password, if considering hidden names and passwords as if on a computer or a smart phone. The hidden password: this information is presented in VERSE 18. But would the name used for this example have any indications to support this random possibility of being that person described as the false prophet? Let's consider if he has any of those tendencies.

For expediency let's use a convenient list that Joshua Riddle at youngconservatives.com posted on October 2, 2013 about Obama's religious statements regarding Islam. Riddle's article is titled '40 mind-blowing quotes from Barack Obama about Islam and Christianity' but only the first quotes will be shown here. Riddle begins, "This is a great list highlighting how radical President Obama is when it comes to Islam and Christianity:"

#1 "The future must not belong to those who slander the Prophet of Islam."

#2 "The sweetest sound I know is the Muslim call to prayer."

#3 "We will convey our deep appreciation for the Islamic faith, which has done so much over the centuries to shape the world — including in my own country."

#4 "As a student of history, I also know civilization's debt to Islam."

#5 "Islam has a proud tradition of tolerance."

#6 "Islam has always been part of America."

#7 "We will encourage more Americans to study in Muslim communities."

#8 "These rituals remind us of the principles that we hold in common, and Islam's role in advancing justice, progress, tolerance, and the dignity of all human beings."

#9 "America and Islam are not exclusive and need not be in competition. Instead, they overlap, and share common principles of justice and progress, tolerance and the dignity of all human beings."

#10 "I made clear that America is not – and never will be – at war with Islam."

#11 "Islam is not part of the problem in combating violent extremism – it is an important part of promoting peace."

#12 "So I have known Islam on three continents before coming to the region where it was first revealed."

#13 "In ancient times and in our times, Muslim communities have been at the forefront of innovation and education."

#14 "Throughout history, Islam has demonstrated through words and deeds the possibilities of religious tolerance and racial equality."

#15 "Ramadan is a celebration of a faith known for great diversity and racial equality."

#16 "The Holy Koran tells us, 'O mankind! We have created you male and a female; and we have made you into nations and tribes so that you may know one another.'"

#17 "I look forward to hosting an Iftar dinner celebrating Ramadan here at the White House later this week, and wish you a blessed month."

#18 "We've seen those results in generations of Muslim immigrants – farmers and factory workers, helping to lay the railroads and build our cities, the Muslim innovators who helped build some of our highest skyscrapers and who helped unlock the secrets of our universe."

#19 "That experience guides my conviction that partnership between America and Islam must be based on what Islam is, not what it isn't. And I consider it part of my responsibility as president of the United States to fight against negative stereotypes of Islam wherever they appear."

#20 "I also know that Islam has always been a part of America's story."

Now let's examine what Obama says about the Christian religion:

At a fundraiser in San Francisco, in April, 2008, he said, "You go into these small towns in Pennsylvania and, like a lot of small towns in the Midwest, the jobs have been gone now for 25 years and nothing's replaced them. And they fell through the Clinton administration, and the Bush administration, and each successive administration has said that somehow these communities are gonna regenerate and they have not.

And it's not surprising then they get bitter, they cling to guns or religion or antipathy toward people who aren't like them or anti-immigrant sentiment or anti-trade sentiment as a way to explain their frustrations." Should guns and religion be compared in that way? His reference to religion was aiming at Christianity, the dominant religion in those areas. Likely, most Christians would consider these comments and these comparisons as 'blasphemy.'

On September 7, 2008, during an interview with George Stephanopoulos, he referenced, "My Muslim faith." If he is a Muslim, why does he continue to deny it?

When speaking of the Koran, he says, "The Holy Koran." When referencing the Bible, he says, "The Bible." Why does he consider the Koran holy and the Bible not holy?

On June 28, 2006, during his 'Call to Renewal' speech, he mocked three sections of the Bible, including the Sermon on the Mount, which he called 'so radical.' He asked, mockingly, "Can either of these be used to guide public policy?" Both the comments and the comparisons would certainly be considered 'blasphemy' against God and Christianity.

On April 16, 2009, he required the monogram for the name of Jesus be covered before he made his speech at Georgetown University. The monogram above an archway was covered with black painted plywood. Certainly he would not consider this blasphemy - black painted plywood covering the symbol of Jesus. Has he such little respect for Christianity that he would make his blasphemy and his disregard for the religion that conspicuous?

The list of Obama's anti-Christian actions, rhetoric, and blasphemies is too long to identify each individually. A casual review of his actions and comments against churches, especially the Catholic Church, Defense of Marriage Act, cabinet appointments, and exclusion of Christian leaders from religious events are clear proof that he has no respect for God, Christian values, or any reference to the value foundation that allowed the formation of our great country - The United States of America.

In my search, I have found nothing Obama has said positive about God or the Christian religion. He has never said a negative word about the Muslim religion.

What are his intentions for the United States and the world. Does he have a preassigned destiny? Are his actions as destructive to our nation and the good world, as are his words?

Chapter 5
The Four Horses

Those four horses of the Apocalypse are often mentioned in casual religious conversation, or as a glib comment referring to Revelation. Most people have heard of these horses, especially that dastardly pale horse who brings Death, and Hell follows.

Revelation, Chapter 5, explains the introduction and importance of the book with Seven Seals which God held in His hand on His throne. John was saddened because 'no man was found worthy to open the book, and to read the book, neither to look thereon.' Finally, John was told by an elder, "Weep not: behold, the Lion of Juda, the Root of David, hath prevailed to open the book and to loose the seven seals thereof."

John was surprised when from the large assembly around the throne, the elders and the four beasts, rose a Lamb as it had been slain. The Lamb was described as "having seven horns and seven eyes, which are the seven Spirits of God sent forth into all the earth." These seven Spirits are mentioned many times throughout Revelation. The Lamb, Jesus, was the only one strong enough to open the seven seals of that book. Opening of the first four seals gave a description of four horses. They are the white horse, the red horse, the black horse, and the pale horse. Let's begin with the white horse, the meaning of which is often misinterpreted.

The White Horse

When he opened the first seal, the first beast invited John to "Come and see." That first beast is not described in this chapter. He had been described in an earlier chapter, Chapter 4, as 'like a lion.' Perhaps this was a representation of the Lion of Judah. What did John see? "And I saw, and behold, a white horse; and he that sat on him had a bow; and a crown was given unto him; and he went forth conquering, and to conquer."

This is the only mention of the white horse in this chapter, leaving many to suggest this was a description of the antichrist, because he had a bow. Some interpret this as a weapon bow. Later it's described as a rainbow. Some also recognize that the white horse described in Chapter 19, is not the same white horse introduced in Chapter 6. Further reading and research suggest it is the same white horse. The introductions are separated because of the differing conditions and purposes. Chapter 19, beginning with Verse11 which announced the preparation for that final great battle. It reads:

"And I saw heaven opened, and behold a white horse; and he that sat upon his was called Faithful and True, and in righteousness he doth judge and make war. 12) His eyes were as a flame of fire, and on his head were many crowns; and he had a name written, that no man knew, but he himself. 13) And he was clothed with a vesture dipped in blood; and his name is called The Word of God. 14) And the armies which were in heaven followed him upon white horses, clothed in fine linen, white and clean."

The Red Horse

When He opened the second seal, the second beast told John, "Come and see." This second beast, described in Chapter 4, was 'like a calf.' This rider was the one to be killed in that final great battle. Perhaps this calf was a representation of one to be slaughtered, in the end. Verse 4 continues, "and there went out another horse that was red; and power was given to him that sat thereon to take peace from the earth, and that they should kill one another; and there was given unto him a great sword." More information about the rider of the red horse gets really interesting and complicated - about killing one another. Let's examine that additional information presented in Chapter 17.

Chapter 17 begins with an angel inviting John to "Come hither; I will shew unto thee the judgment of the great whore that sitteth upon many waters: 2) With whom the kings of the earth have committed fornication, and the inhabitants of the earth have been made drunk with the wine of her fornication." There, John saw a woman (already described as that religion Islam) sit upon a scarlet colored beast (that red horse) full of names of blasphemy. As explained earlier in this writing, Verses 5 and 6 clearly identify this woman as Islam. Understanding that, then one can interpret the meaning of Verse 4, which precedes those verses. This is more significant than gleaned at first glance:

"And the woman was arrayed in purple and scarlet colour, and decked with gold and precious stones and pearls, having a golden cup in her hand full of abominations and filthiness of her fornication."

The significance of this verse has never been described before. Simply, it means Islam had a golden cup full of precious oil that was the source of power that the world depended on. The worship of that source created acceptance of Islam's abominations and fornication. Is this a surprise? Just to make sure this concept is understood, it's repeated and made clearer in Chapter 18, Verses 15-17:

"The merchants of these things, which were made rich by her, shall stand afar off for the fear of torment, weeping and wailing, And saying , Alas, alas that great city (Babylon-Islam) that was clothed in fine linen, and purple, and scarlet, and decked with gold, and precious stones, and pearls! For in one hour so great riches is come to nought."

The colors red and scarlet are described in both similar references. Red and scarlet are the derivative colors of amber - which is the natural color of oil. These are descriptions of things to happen during that great war. Muslim's oil resources will be destroyed. This destruction helps create the introduction of the black horse, next.

The Black Horse

When he opened the third seal, the third beast having 'a face as a man' said, "Come and see." John observed, "And I beheld, and lo a black horse; and he that sat on him had a pair of balances in his hand. And I heard a voice in the midst of the four beasts say, 'A penny, and three measures of barley for a penny; and see thou hurt not the oil and the wine.'"

Clearly, this is a description of the normal subsistence problems of mankind during and after these battles and these tribulations caused by the rider of the red horse; the one that will take peace from the earth. This is understanding of course that the rider of the red horse is not just a single person, but instead representing a certain influence. For example, if oil supplies are cut off from the turmoil areas such as the Middle-East, what problems would that create for those Islamic nations as well as normal world commerce? Let's review with more information in Chapter 18. That information begins with Verse 3:

"For all nations have drunk of the wine of the wrath of her fornication, and the kings of the earth have committed fornication with her, and the merchants of the earth are waxed rich through the abundance of her delicacies." This verse introduces difficult times ahead especially for citizens of those oil-producing countries, as well as merchants of the world who have relied on that oil to make themselves rich. Those conditions are detailed in the next verses. The first is an appeal for God's people to remove themselves from that fornication, and "that ye be not partakers of her sins, and that ye receive not her plagues." Then the judgment of those nations continues with Verse 5:

"For her sins have reached unto heaven, and God hath remembered her iniquities. 6) Reward her even as she rewarded you, and double unto her double according to her works: in the cup which she hath filled fill to her double. 7) How much she hath glorified herself, and lived deliciously, so much torment and sorrow give her; for she saith in her heart, I sit a queen, and am no widow, and shall see no sorrow. 8) Therefore shall her plagues come in one day, death, and mourning, and famine; and she shall be utterly burned with fire; for strong is the Lord God who judgeth her." Let's pause here and consider.

Granted, this seems a harsh judgment; and that judgment seems to be taken by God's hand. Several things are important to piece together to create understanding of this concept. First, consider the depth and severity of her (Islam's) sins? 'Her sins have reached unto heaven.' Those sinners are challenging God directly. So, what is the reaction? This is the time to recall that those seven Spirits live inside everyone who accepts the Word of God. Those Spirits inside us include power and strength. That power and strength is to do God's will. Now, let's consider why God chose to take that action through the Spirit of his people.

Chapter 18, Verse 24 reports the severity of their acts against God, "And in her was found the blood of prophets, and of saints, and of all that were slain upon the earth." Then, the reactions are given in Chapter 19, beginning with Verse 11: "And I saw heaven opened, and behold a white horse; and he that sat upon him was called Faithful and True, and in righteousness he doth judge and make war. 12) His eyes were as a flame of fire, and on his head were many crowns; and he had a name written, that no man knew, but he himself. 13) And he was clothed with a vesture dipped in blood: and his name is called The Word of God. 14) And the armies which were in heaven followed him upon white horses, clothed in fine linen, white and clean."

After that the results of the great battle are stated. Perhaps those other riders on white horses are those guided by God's Spirit from within to do that physical battle. What will happen throughout the world when that great battle begins? That's the beginning of the tribulation period, as explained, beginning with Chapter 18,Verse 9:

"And the kings of the earth, who have committed fornication and lived deliciously with her, shall bewail her, and lament for her, when they shall see the smoke of her burning, 10) Standing afar off for the fear of her torment, saying, Alas, alas that great city of Babylon, that mighty city! For in one hour is thy judgment come." Then, the next several verses give enough examples to show that world trade and commerce as we now know it will come to a halt. Verse 11 begins to show the agony of those involved with that commerce:

"And the merchants of the earth shall weep and mourn over her; for no man buyeth their merchandise any more: 12) The merchandise of gold, and silver, and precious stones, and of pearls, and fine linen, and purple, and silk, and scarlet, and all thyine wood, and all manner vessels of ivory, and all manner vessels of most precious wood, and of brass, and iron, and marble." Verses 13 and 14 continue with a long list of other items that will no longer be available for commerce. Before we go further, let's consider that most important item - oil. It's mentioned here, above, again in the form of 'purple' and 'scarlet.' And, this verse is not the last mention of those colors. Verse 16 repeats that importance, after Verse 15 reveals the merchants' despair:

"And saying, Alas, alas that great city, that was clothed in fine linen, and purple, and scarlet, and decked with gold, and precious stones, and pearls!" The next verse, 17, gives the major clue for the lack of world commerce; it's the absence of ships and transportation, probably oil to propel those vehicles of commerce:

"For in one hour so great riches is come to nought. And every shipmaster, and all the company in ships, and sailors, and as many as trade by sea, stood afar off, 18) And cried when they saw the smoke of her burning, saying, What city is like unto this great city!" Now, if that's not punishment enough, God goes even further in his destruction of that great city - Islam. That explanation begins in Verse 20:

"Rejoice over her, thou heaven, and ye holy apostles and prophets; for Got hath avenged you on her. 21) And a mighty angel took up a stone like a great millstone, and cast it into the sea, (sea of mankind) saying, Thus with violence shall that great city Babylon be thrown down, and shall be found no more at all." Now, this presents the question: to whom was he speaking? Chapter 6, Verses 9-11, answers this question:

"And when he had opened the fifth seal, I saw under the alter the souls of them that were slain for the word of God, and for the testimony which they held: 10) An they cried with a loud voice, saying, How long O Lord, holy and true, dost thou not judge and avenge our blood on them that dwell on the earth? 11) And white robes were given unto every one of them; and it was said unto them, that they should rest yet for a little season, until their fellowservants also and their brethren, that should be killed as they were, should be killed." This second group to be killed referred to those who were killed by refusing the mark of the beast, as explained in Chapter 13.

Then, returning to Chapter 19, verses 23 and 24 give the conclusion to this part of the Apocalypse:

"And the light of a candle shall shine no more at all in thee; and the voice of the bridegroom and of the bride shall be heard no more at all in thee; for the merchants were the great men of the earth; for by thy sorceries were all nations deceived. 24) And in her was found the blood of the prophets, and of saints, and of all that were slain upon the earth." This is the same blood that identified Babylon as Islam in Verse 6 of Chapter 17. "Alas, alas; Babylon has fallen, has fallen."

The Pale Horse

The rider of the pale horse is the one most feared by readers of Revelation. This horse represents pure and simple death. When the fourth seal was opened, the fourth beast 'like a flying eagle' said, "Come and see." John continued with his observations:

"And I looked, and behold a pale horse; and his name that sat on him was Death, and Hell followed with him. And power was given unto them over the fourth part of the earth, to kill with sword, and with hunger, and with death, and with the beasts of the earth." Perhaps the beast, the 'one like an eagle' represents widespread disasters, covering many parts of the earth.

Although the later parts of Revelation give no specific details introduced by opening the fourth seal, there have been historical disasters so great that they must apply to this revelation. Three specifics are: sword, hunger, and with the beasts. Although there are no precise historical statistics proving a quarter of the earth's population was killed by the rider of the pale horse, data certainly suggest at least that many were killed in one great incident; the Black Death, during the 1300s. And throughout history, many have been slaughtered by the sword; those weapons of war.

Certainly the greatest beginning of slaughter by the sword was during the Crusades from 1095 through 1271. This is approximately the same time the Europeans left the Holy Land and other parts of the Middle East, allowing Islam to rise and flourish, beginning in Mecca.

Next came the deaths during World War 1. There were 10 million military personnel and 7 million civilians killed during that time with military weaponry (swords.) Beasts (diseases - especially the Spanish flu) caused about a third of those deaths.

According to Wikipedia, more deaths resulted from WWII than from any war in history. A little more than 60 million people were killed in that conflict; although high in number it was just a little over three percent of the world population at that time. Including disease and famine from the conflict, the total death number exceeded 80 million.

The greatest percentage of population deaths in history was caused by a disease (beast) known as the Black Death. An article from historytoday.com, by Ole J. Benedictow gives those specific details. The article is titled: Black Death Greatest Catastrophe Ever. It was published in History Today Volume 55 Issue 3 March 2005:

"Ole J. Benedictow describes how he calculated that the Black Death killed 50 million people in the 14th century, or 60 per cent of Europe's entire population:

The disastrous mortal disease known as the Black Death spread across Europe in the years 1346-53. The frightening name, however, only came several centuries after its visitation (and was probably a mistranslation of the Latin word 'atra' meaning both 'terrible' and 'black)'. Chronicles and letters from the time describe the terror wrought by the illness. In Florence, the great Renaissance poet Petrarch was sure that they would not be believed: 'O happy posterity, who will not experience such abysmal woe and will look upon our testimony as a fable.' A Florentine chronicler relates that:

'All the citizens did little else except to carry dead bodies to be buried. At every church they dug deep pits down to the water-table; and thus those who were poor who died during the night were bundled up quickly and thrown into the pit. In the morning when a large number of bodies were found in the pit, they took some earth and shoveled it down on top of them; and later others were placed on top of them and then another layer of earth, just as one makes lasagna with layers of pasta and cheese.

The accounts are remarkably similar. The chronicler Agnolo di Tura 'the Fat' relates from his Tuscan home town that:

"... in many places in Siena great pits were dug and piled deep with the multitude of dead. And there were also those who were so sparsely covered with earth that the dogs dragged them forth and devoured many bodies throughout the city."

The tragedy was extraordinary. In the course of just a few months, 60 percent of Florence's population died from the plague, and probably the same proportion in Siena. In addition to the bald statistics, we come across profound personal tragedies: Petrarch lost to the Black Death his beloved Laura to whom he wrote his famous love poems; Di Tura tells us that 'I buried my five children with my own hands.'

The Black Death was an epidemic of bubonic plague, a disease caused by the bacterium Yersinia pestis that circulates among wild rodents where they live in great numbers and density. Such an area is called a 'plague focus' or a 'plague reservoir'. Plague among humans arises when rodents in human habitation, normally black rats, become infected. The black rat, also called the 'house rat' and the 'ship rat', likes to live close to people, the very quality that makes it dangerous (in contrast, the brown or grey rat prefers to keep its distance in sewers and cellars).

Normally, it takes ten to fourteen days before plague has killed off most of a contaminated rat colony, making it difficult for great numbers of fleas gathered on the remaining, but soon-dying, rats to find new hosts. After three days of fasting, hungry rat fleas turn on humans. From the bite site, the contagion drains to a lymph node that consequently swells to form a painful bubo, most often in the groin, on the thigh, in an armpit or on the neck. Hence the name bubonic plague. The infection takes three–five days to incubate in people before they fall ill, and another three–five days before, in 80 per cent of the cases, the victims die. Thus, from the introduction of plague contagion among rats in a human community it takes, on average, twenty-three days before the first person dies.

When, for instance, a stranger called Andrew Hogson died from plague on his arrival in Penrith in 1597, and the next plague case followed twenty-two days later, this corresponded to the first phase of the development of an epidemic of bubonic plague. And Hobson was, of course, not the only fugitive from a plague-stricken town or area arriving in various communities in the region with infective rat fleas in their clothing or luggage. This pattern of spread is called 'spread by leaps' or 'metastatic spread'. Thus, plague soon broke out in other urban and rural centres, from where the disease spread into the villages and townships of the surrounding districts by a similar process of leaps.

In order to become an epidemic the disease must be spread to other rat colonies in the locality and transmitted to inhabitants in the same way. It took some time for people to recognize that a terrible epidemic was breaking out among them and for chroniclers to note this. The timescale varies: in the countryside it took about forty days for realisation to dawn; in most towns with a few thousand inhabitants, six to seven weeks; in the cities with over 10,000 inhabitants, about seven weeks, and in the few metropolises with over 100,000 inhabitants, as much as eight weeks.

Plague bacteria can break out of the buboes and be carried by the blood stream to the lungs and cause a variant of plague that is spread by contaminated droplets from the cough of patients (pneumonic plague). However, contrary to what is sometimes believed, this form is not contracted easily, spreads normally only episodically or incidentally and constitutes therefore normally only a small fraction of plague cases. It now appears clear that human fleas and lice did not contribute to the spread, at least not significantly. The bloodstream of humans is not invaded by plague bacteria from the buboes, or people die with so few bacteria in the blood that bloodsucking human parasites become insufficiently infected to become infective and spread the disease: the blood of plague-infected rats contains 500-1,000 times more bacteria per unit of measurement than the blood of plague-infected humans.

Importantly, plague was spread considerable distances by rat fleas on ships. Infected ship rats would die, but their fleas would often survive and find new rat hosts wherever they landed. Unlike human fleas, rat fleas are adapted to riding with their hosts; they readily also infest clothing of people entering affected houses and ride with them to other houses or localities. This gives plague epidemics a peculiar rhythm and pace of development and a characteristic pattern of dissemination. The fact that plague is transmitted by rat fleas means plague is a disease of the warmer seasons, disappearing during the winter, or at least lose most of their powers of spread. The peculiar seasonal pattern of plague has been observed everywhere and is a systematic feature also of the spread of the Black Death.

In the plague history of Norway from the Black Death 1348-49 to the last outbreaks in 1654, comprising over thirty waves of plague, there was never a winter epidemic of plague. Plague is very different from airborne contagious diseases, which are spread directly between people by droplets: these thrive in cold weather.

This conspicuous feature constitutes proof that the Black Death and plague in general is an insect-borne disease. Cambridge historian John Hatcher has noted that there is 'a remarkable transformation in

the seasonal pattern of mortality in England after 1348: whilst before the Black Death the heaviest mortality was in the winter months, in the following century it was heaviest in the period from late July to late September. He points out that this strongly indicates that the 'transformation was caused by the virulence of bubonic plague.'
End of the History Today article.

The rider of the pale horse also represented death by hunger. No better example of death by hunger than is in Africa - historically and today. Missionariesofafrica.org submitted the following article explaining that dire and devastating situation. The article begins:

"Results from a recent study of current living conditions throughout Africa report that more than one billion people do not have enough clean water to provide for their basic human needs. As a result, more than 2,500 children are dying each day.

"When people are desperately thirsty," one official explained, "they are willing to take the risk of disease by consuming water that may not be healthy. For them - it's either risk infection or die from thirst! It is a horrible position to be in."

Unsafe drinking water can carry diseases such as malaria, trypanosomiasis, intestinal worm infections, dengue, and schistosomiasis - as well as bacteria that can lead to deadly diarrheal infections. "In some areas," the report continued, "the level of suffering and misery owing to the inadequacy of clean water is almost beyond comprehension judging by the number of pregnant women and children who suffer from deadly diarrheal diseases such as cholera and dysentery.

"These parasites and diseases feed on very young children and the elderly," explains Fr. Richard Roy. Fr. Roy is the director of the Missionaries of Africa's development office in Washington, DC. "They are the innocent and silent members of society... they have no one to be a voice for them."

"Entire villages and communities are being wiped out by diseases that are living in dirty water," Fr. Roy continued. "Children are dying in huge numbers! For many people, these numbers are so big that they cannot begin to comprehend them - they are statistics! But imagine your own child dying . . . and then imagine if it happened to every child in your neighborhood school! That's when we start to understand how horrible the crisis is! These poor people desperately need our help!" The Missionaries of Africa are currently accepting contributions that will be used to provide safe drinking water for men, women and children in Africa's neediest regions. All donations are tax-deductible.

Drought! Devastating drought is once again threatening the lives of African men, women and children. In the months ahead, as many as 14 million people will be at risk of starvation and malnutrition.

"Vegetation has decreased drastically," a study on the current conditions within the African continent recently stated. "The eastern side of the continent on the Horn of Africa is being affected more substantially than others. In this region, the rainy season occurs between February and June. Much less rain has fallen than normal this year, so their staple crops of corn and sorghum simply withered. Poor harvests over the past three years have worn away food surpluses and incomes in the region. As many as 14 million people may be at risk of malnutrition or starvation." The study stated that as much as 270,000 metric tons of food assistance will be needed immediately; but only 120,000 metric tons is currently available.

"Food shortages are particularly severe in eastern and southern Ethiopia," another report explained, "where deaths from starvation are being increasingly reported. Sudan and Uganda are also being affected."

"We are seeing an entire continent of people experience suffering like never before!" explains Fr. Richard Roy who served in Africa as a missionary for more than 20 years before being assigned to head the organization's development office in Washington, DC. "With a drought of this magnitude -- the land, the animals, the people -- everything is dying! If we don't reach out - we could see the end of entire villages, regions . . . even cities. An enormous amount of food, water and medicine is needed. I am praying that our benefactors will help us get supplies to our missionaries in the field . . . so that they can reach those who are on the verge of dying!" End of article.

The incidents of massive deaths in the past, from war, starvation, and pestilence have been examples of what could lie ahead in our future. Great battles in Africa and the Middle East, especially involving nuclear weapons, could make those past deaths from the 'rider on the pale horse' seem very minor. That great war has been prophesied.

Many followers of Christ have already been slaughtered in the past. What happened to their souls? The next chapter, the opening of the fifth seal explains.

Chapter Six
The Fifth Seal

The four horsemen were introduced when the first four seals of the seven seals were broken. When the next three seals were broken John saw only the events that occurred when they were released. There were no other riders of other horses. He continued his vision of those events he saw:

Chapter 6, Verse 9, "And when he had opened the fifth seal, I saw under the alter the souls of them that were slain for the word of God, and for the testimony which they held: 10) And they cried with a loud voice, saying, How long, O Lord, holy and true, dost thou not judge and avenge our blood on them that dwell on the earth?11) And white robes were given unto every one of them; and it was said unto them, that they should rest yet for a little season, until their fellow servants also and their brethren, that should be killed as they were, should be fulfilled."

Although this fifth seal might seem less important than the first four, it holds great significance; it's related to two other events that might not be understood without this information. First, it explains how these waiting souls are different from those who will be killed for refusing that 'mark of the beast.' Second, it's the basis of differentiation between the first resurrection and the second resurrection. That mark is described in Chapter 13.

Chapter 13 explains the formal introduction of the beast as a world leader or conqueror. The common understanding for the name of this beast is the 'Antichrist.' However, that name is never used in the Book of Revelation; only the 'beast.' He's introduced in Verse 2 as being like a leopard, and his feet of a bear, and his mouth as a lion; "and the dragon gave him his power, and his seat, and great authority," when he rose from the sea. Generally, in Revelation, sea refers to the sea of humanity, not from a watery sea. The beast could also be interpreted as the religion or the following of that actual physical beast, that person.

Perhaps he's perceived as a leopard because of his stealth; a leopard is a cat that hunts by stealth and surprise. In many places in the Bible, particularly Revelation, the beast is described as deceptive; as well as blasphemous. Deception could be considered a form of stealth to ensnare believers influenced by the dragon to accept his 'peaceful' methods.

Another reference describes the beast as 'stout.' Perhaps that's the source of 'feet of a bear.' He's relentless in his approach, and speaks dark and persuasive phrases. A lion is known for its great roar. The beast is described as having a forceful voice with strong persuasions. He's so stout and persuasive that many will worship the dragon and will follow the beast, asking 'Who can make war with him?'

Although the beast has a serious wound to his head and arm many will follow him to make war against the 'saints.' The saints being those on earth who follow the Word of God. All those whose names are not written in the 'Book of Life' will follow him. According to Verse 5, "...and power was given unto him to continue 'forty and two months.' That's three and a half years. (Notice the time, two times, and a half time again.) Other information in this book identifies Muhammad, the one who claimed to be higher than Christ, as that first beast. Verse 10 suggests the death of Muhammad: "He that killeth with the sword must be killed with the sword."

Chapter 13 continues and says a second beast will arise having the same powers as had the first beast, and he will promote the first beast; since the first beast had a 'deadly head wound that was healed.' That was the source of much of his accepted power. Since many thought he had been killed, and he rose again, they believed he was the risen Savior. They accepted him as higher than Christ; which is the source of the word 'antichrist.' Antichrist means in the place of Christ; not someone against Christ. That's why he's so popular and accepted; many true believers will be deceived. That false belief will cost them their salvation.

Once accepted, the second beast will have an image to the first beast built. Verse 15 adds, "And he had power to give life unto the image of the beast, that the image of the beast should both speak and cause as many as would not worship the image of the beast should be killed." What is the normal interpretation of this verse; the interpretation I held for several years? This statement is one I wrote just recently that explains:

"This is likely a computer or a hologram; when John wrote this he could only see the vision. He would not have understood a computer or a hologram." Now, I have abandoned that interpretation, due to the events now happening in the Middle East and throughout the world. It gives great difference in the meanings and proposals of two small words: To and Of.

I've been reading and writing something about Revelation every day since Barack Obama was re-elected; trying to understand how something that horrible could happen to the future of America and the world. Often, I think I have something properly interpreted, then it turns around and slaps me in the face. Just yesterday I realized that the two words of 'to' and 'of' present a totally different story. That's in reference to that image of the beast in Chapter13, Verse14:

"...that they should make an image to the beast, which had the wound by a sword, and did live."

First, let's consider the beast that had the wound 'and did live.' This describes Muhammad, the beast also described in other parts of the Bible as the antichirst; he placed himself above Christ. Muhammad, leading warriors from Medina, was thought to have been killed in the Battle of Uhud against the Meccans in 625 AD. He was struck in the face by three arrows and his front teeth were knocked out by a stone. He fell as dead on the battlefield. Later he rose and joined his Meccan forces who had retreated. His recovery was considered a miracle.

Most, including myself, have interpreted the image as an image 'of' the beast. The verse says 'to' the beast. In reality that first interpretation should not have been considered, anyway, since Islam does not allow an image to be made 'of' the beast. So, what might this mean?

Is it possible that we are living the Apocalypse today? We have a new caliphate now in the Middle East; is that not an image TO the beast? Those people within that caliphate region are killed if they don't have the mark of the beast - accept Islam either in their thoughts (their foreheads) or in their hands by using weapons against others? Is Obama's refusal to destroy them not encouragement that they 'should make an image to the beast?'

And we shouldn't forget to 'count the number' of a man; the beast which is 666. That equals 18. And, that's confirmed with this information being in Verse 18. Now, who do we know whose full name has 18 letters. And, he's the man that has the current power to perform miracles; like making fire come down from the sky in the form of rockets, bombs, and missiles.

The word 'beast' also gets complicated. Muhammad was the first beast. The second beast, also known as the false prophet, is the one whom 18:16: says, "causeth all...to receive a mark." He doesn't create the mark - but he allows it 'causeth' it to happen with certain actions, words, and inactions.

Chapter 14 seems to announce a stern warning to those who accept the mark of the beast and follow him, instead of adhering to those signs to repent. Verse 6 begins that final warning. The sequence of events for that final warning is unclear; since each chapter and verse in Revelation does not follow in a straight or direct pattern. The information is all interspersed and seems out of pattern, place, or position. This was written from John's vision; perhaps he wrote as he remembered the scenes from those visions. Nevertheless, Verse 6 begins a stern warning:

"And I saw another angel fly in the midst of heaven, having the everlasting gospel to preach unto them that dwell on the earth, and to every nation, and kindred, and tongue, and people, Saying with a loud voice, Fear God, and give glory to him; for the hour of his judgment is come: and worship him that made heaven, and earth, and the sea, and the fountains of waters."

Verse 8 continues, "And there followed another angel saying, Babylon is fallen, is fallen, that great city, because she made all nations drink of the wine of the wrath of her fornication.(Remember here that 'she' Babylon is the identification of that religion, Islam; not a physical city.)

Verse 9, "And the third angel followed them, saying with a loud voice, If any man worship the beast and his image, and receive his mark in his forehead, or in his hand, The same shall drink of the wine of the wrath of God, which is poured out without mixture into the cup of his indignation; and he shall be tormented with fire and brimstone in the presence of the holy angels, and in the presence of the Lamb."

The remainder of Chapter 14 applies to the next broken seal. The next verse that applies to this, the fifth seal, continues in Chapter 20, after the first real battle between the forces of evil and good.

Chapter 20, Verse 4: "And I saw thrones and they sat upon them, and judgment was given unto them; and I saw the souls of them that were beheaded for the witness of Jesus and for the word of God, and which had not worshiped the beast, neither his image, neither had received his mark upon their foreheads, or in their hands; and they lived and reigned with Christ a thousand years. 5) But the rest of the dead lived not again (this includes those waiting under the alter who asked when they would be avenged) until the thousand years were finished. This is the first resurrection. 6) Blessed and holy is he that hath part in the first resurrection; on such the second death hath no power, but they shall be priests of God and of Christ, and shall reign with him a thousand years." ('The second death hath no power' means their names don't have to be considered from the final book of life. They are already in heaven.)

Verse 7 makes another serious admonition: "And when the thousand years are expired, Satan shall be loosed out of his prison." This thousand years of peace is commonly known as the Millennium. Verse 8 explains what happens after that thousand years, "And shall go out to deceive the nations which are in the four quarters of the earth, Gog and Ma'gog, to gather them together to battle; the number of whom is as the sand of the sea." Verses 9 and 10 are included in this position but might be better placed after all the information about the impending great battle; however since it's part of this discussion, it will be included here:

"And they went up on the breadth of the earth, and compassed the camp of the saints about, and the beloved city; and fire came down from God out of heaven and devoured them." In this scene, perhaps as the large army of Satan gathered on the high ground around Jerusalem before their great attack, they were destroyed by fire; likely a surprise nuclear attack; perhaps from a country that had not been as destroyed as had been Israel. Maybe even from the United States?

Verse 10 gives the finality of Satan: "And the devil that deceived them was cast into the lake of fire and brimstone, where the beast and the false prophet (the second beast) are;" where they remained forever."

Then everyone, every soul, was judged from the 'book of life' according to their works. This was the second resurrection. It was the resurrection for all those souls who had been waiting under the alter, and all their fellow servants who followed them. The first resurrection had been for those beheaded because they refused to accept the mark of the beast. Verse 15: "And whosoever was not found written in the book of life was cast into the lake of fire," along with death and hell who had been mentioned in the previous verse.

Perhaps this is a good time to mention the 'Rapture.' The rapture is never mentioned in the Bible - at any place. The only ones who will be taken up to reign with God in the final years are those who refused to accept the mark. Their souls will be taken up, not their physical bodies and souls. Nobody will be standing in a crowd and suddenly disappear into heaven to avoid the tribulation that will last forty-two months (three and a half years) when Jerusalem is occupied by the beast: the Abomination of Desolation.

Iran, and other Islamic countries suggest that Israel should not exist and should be 'wiped off the face of the earth.' That great attack is coming. Everyone has been warned to reject the subtleties of the beast. John warned the seven churches of Asia - and us - "Those who have an ear - pay attention."

Chapter Seven
The Sixth Seal

C hapter 6, Verses 12-14: "And I beheld when he had opened the sixth seal, and, lo, there was a great earthquake; and the sun became black as sackcloth of hair, and the moon became as blood; And the stars of heaven fell unto the earth, even as a fig tree casteth her untimely figs, when she is shaken of a mighty wind. And the heaven departed as a scroll when it is rolled together; and every mountain and island were moved out of their places."

(As an interesting side note, one might ask why John mentioned stars falling from heaven, 'even as a fig tree casteth her untimely figs, when she is shaken of a mighty wind' in Verse 13. The answer: When Jesus was crucified, He appointed John as the guardian for His mother, Mary. John took care of her and even carried her to his last place of worship and teaching; the church at Ephesus. He was exiled to Patmos while he was at Ephesus, and returned to Ephesus when he was released from exile. At that time he was thought to be almost a hundred years old. Before he was exiled, he left Mary in a small home on a hill that overlooks the now ruins of Ephesus. Her home was surrounded by many large fig trees - perhaps the association with his words about fig trees. The buried foundation of the house was discovered from a vision by a blind Catholic Nun named Catherine Emmerich. She never left her native Germany, but directed others from her vision. She is also recognized for many other great prophetic visions. More information about the house can be found at: House of the Virgin Mary in Wikipedia and other internet locations.)

This was the beginning of many great earthly natural disasters to warn those who worshiped the beast to turn from him and accept the mercy of the Lord. As are the other parts of information from the opened seals, these parts are also scattered and interspersed throughout the words in Revelation. Possibly John wrote his visions as he remembered them, and they weren't all displayed in a direct sequentially related order.

Some were natural disasters, some were created from man's misuse of the ecology, and some resulted from vicious warfare. The verses immediately following the opening of the sixth seal give an overview of those disasters, such as a topic sentence in a paragraph. That overview is included in Verses 12-17. They mention stars falling unto the earth, heaven departing as a scroll, and every mountain and island being moved out of their places. It also mentions how all men, rich and poor, hid in the rocks during those earthquakes and asked to be hidden from the one who sitteth on the throne, and from the wrath of the Lamb. It concludes: "For the great day of his wrath is come and who shall be able to stand." Perhaps the non-believers began to realize their fallacy, but still refused to abandon the beast and accept God.

The mention of 'the sun became black as sackcloth of hair, and the moon became as blood' in verse 4 refers to darkening skies from many sources; including volcanic eruptions, bombs exploding, and even the results of great smoke from massive artillery fire. It could even be from much wood being burned for heat during the tribulation period, when normal power sources might be minimized, delayed, or even destroyed. This time of tribulation could last from three and a half years to seven years. How much wood would have to be burned; how many trees would have to be cut down to provide heat to a cold world? Would that not create enough smoke to darken the moon and the sun?

Of course, many stars as we understand stars would not fall onto the earth. Only one star would obliterate the whole planet - before it even reached the earth. Most references to stars in Revelation refer to people or to conditions and influences, and most of those references refer to people of God. Some, however, refer to worshipers of the beast, or even the beast himself.

As in other parts of Revelation, John used great words to describe real and normal events. He was seeing the vision from afar, and at a different time from which he couldn't explain the current names of things to come. Perfect examples are 'an image that speaks' and 'fire from the sky' referring to computers and holograms; and rockets and missiles, in Chapter 13.

Chapter 6, Verse 14 describes, "And, the heaven departed as a scroll when it is rolled together; and every mountain and island were moved out of their places." Perhaps John was describing the power of the atomic bomb and the nuclear bomb, not necessarily that all the mountains will be moved. The nuclear testing at Bikini Atoll might be an example of what John saw in his vision: This information is from Wikipedia:

"The size of the Castle Bravo test on 1 March 1954 far exceeded expectations, causing widespread radioactive contamination. The fallout spread traces of radioactive material as far as Australia, India and Japan, and even the United States and parts of Europe. Though organized as a secret test, Castle Bravo quickly became an international incident, prompting calls for a ban on the atmospheric testing of thermonuclear devices.

The nuclear testing at Bikini Atoll program was a series of 23 nuclear devices detonated by the United States between 1946 and 1958 at seven test sites on the reef itself, on the sea, in the air and underwater. The test weapons produced a combined fission yield of 42.2 Mt of explosive power. The testing began with the Operation Crossroads series in July 1946. The Baker test's radioactive contamination of all the target ships was the first case of immediate, concentrated radioactive fallout from a nuclear explosion. Chemist Glenn T. Seaborg, the longest-serving chairman of the Atomic Energy Commission, called Baker "the world's first nuclear disaster."

The United States was in a Cold War Nuclear arms race with the Soviet Union to build bigger and better bombs. The first series of tests over Bikini Atoll was code named Operation Crossroads. Tests Able and Baker performed as expected, but the first device tested as part of Operation Castle, Castle Bravo, was a new design utilizing a dry fuel thermonuclear hydrogen bomb. It was detonated at dawn on March 1, 1954. The 15 megaton nuclear explosion far exceeded the expected yield of 4 to 8 megatons (6Mt predicted), and was about 1,000 times more powerful than each of the atomic bombs dropped on Hiroshima and Nagasaki during World War II. The scientists and military authorities were shocked by the size of the explosion and many of the instruments they had put in place to evaluate the effectiveness of the device were destroyed.

The military authorities and scientists had promised the Bikini Atoll's native residents that they would be able to return home after the nuclear tests. A majority of the island's family heads agreed to leave the island, and most of the residents were moved to the Rongerik Atoll and later to Kili Island. Both locations proved unsuitable to sustaining life, resulting in starvation and requiring the residents to receive ongoing aid. Despite the promises made by authorities, nuclear tests rendered Bikini unfit for habitation, contaminating the soil and water, making subsistence farming and fishing too dangerous.

The United States later paid the islanders and their descendants $2 billion in compensation for damage caused by the nuclear testing program and their displacement from their home island. As of 2014, it may be technically possible for the former residents and their descendants to live on the atoll's islands. But virtually none of those alive today have ever lived on the atoll and very few want to move there." End of Wikipedia article.

The information given about these nuclear explosions on the island is very precise. It closely matches and resembles many of the visions reported by John as he wrote Revelation. Also, imagine John's confusion as he tried to write of all the other disasters such as earthquakes, floods, fires and Islamic desolation that were to take place centuries after he wrote about them. It was probably more difficult for John to write those things than for us, today, to interpret them.

There are two other factors we must not forget regarding this chapter, especially Verse 15, which reveals: "And the kings of the earth and the great men, and the rich men, and the chief captains, and the mighty men, and every bondman and every free man, hid themselves in the dens and in the rocks of the mountains." Do you recall the time when Osama Bin Laden and his leadership escaped from God's forces during those battles in Afghanistan? They escaped by hiding in the rocks of the Bora Bora Mountains. Others following the guidance of the beast also hid themselves in rocks and caves; and they still do today. The same analysis could be considered for the words in Verse 14:

"And the heaven departed as a scroll when it is rolled together; and every mountain and island were move out of their places." This might not only refer to results of nuclear activity and resulting aftermath from water movement; it could also infer something else. Countries and many other earthly monuments keep changing their names and identities according to new maps being drawn throughout the world. Once those new maps are drawn, are they not rolled together 'as a scroll?'

Verses 16 and 17 conclude Chapter 6:

"And said to the mountains and rocks, Fall on us, and hide us from the face of him that sitteth on the throne, and from the wrath of the Lamb; For the great day of the wrath is come; and who shall be able to stand." These are the words of 'the kings of the earth, and the great men, and every man' who hide themselves. When the great battle begins, there will be many who will hide themselves, in the rocks and everywhere, from their despair and shame. But most will 'repent not.'

Clearly, those who continued to defy God with their worship of the beast; that 'mother of harlots who had the blood of the martyrs of Jesus on their swords' knew their worship was in the wrong place. At that time they realized God was taking vengeance against them and their false god - also identified elsewhere as a 'strange' god. That vengeance was represented by angels sounding trumpets and emptying vials of plagues. But as written several times in Revelation: "They repented not." Their resistance continued to bring great tragedy upon them as explained in the next chapter.

The first verse in Chapter 7 is the announcement that dire things are beginning to happen and everyone should prepare. Everything got still; the wind did not blow on the earth, sea, or any tree. Then, Verse 2 explains further:

"And I saw another angel ascending from the east, having the seal of the living God: and he cried with a loud voice to the four angels, to whom it was given to hurt the earth and the sea, 3) Saying, Hurt not the earth, neither the sea, nor the trees, till we have sealed the servants of our God in their foreheads. 4) And I heard the number of them which were sealed: and there were sealed an hundred and forty and fur thousand of all the tribes of the children of Israel."

The next four verses then list twelve thousand from each of those twelve tribes, listed by name, to be converted to Christ, the Lamb. How do we know this conversion takes place? Verses 9 and 10 answer this question: "After this I beheld, and, lo, a great multitude, which no man could number, of all nations, and kindreds, and people, and tongues, stood before the throne, and before the Lamb, clothed with white robes, and palms in their hands; And cried with a loud voice, saying, Salvation to our God which sitteth upon the throne, and unto the Lamb." In summary, they all praised the Lamb; Christ.

The next few verses describe the scene of angels and elders surrounding the throne of God, in worship as they recognize His seven Spirits: blessings, glory, wisdom, thanksgiving, honour, power, and might. After that, one of the elders asked, "What are these which are arrayed in white robes, and whence came they?" Then he replied to John's urging to answer:

"These are they which came out of great tribulation, and have washed their robes, and made them white in the blood of the Lamb." Then he added that they would serve God day and night in his temple: "And he that sitteth on the throne shall dwell among them." Verses 16 and 17 add, "They shall hunger no more, neither thirst any more; neither shall the sun light on them, nor any heat. For the Lamb which is in the midst of the throne shall feed them, and shall lead them unto living fountains of waters: and God shall wipe away all tears from their eyes."

From this above explanation, it seems there will be a long time of tribulation before the deadly wars begin. These will be times of severe atrocities against Christians and Jews by the beast who has developed great power in a certain region, such as in the Middle East, or even worldwide. These standing before the throne, at this time, are those who have been persecuted and martyred during the great tribulation, approximately three and a half years. After that, the actual battles begin. That happens when the seventh seal is opened. The stage was set for horrendous events.

Chapter 8
The Seventh Seal

Many other great disasters occurred when the seventh seal was broken. The first verse of Chapter 8 gave that foreboding as it stated, "And when he had opened the seventh seal, there was silence in heaven about the space of half an hour. 2) And I saw the seven angels which stood before God; and to them were given seven trumpets."

The next verses explained that an angel filled a golden censer with much incense, which was blessed with many saints, filled with the fire of the alter and cast it into the earth. "And there were voices, and thunderings, and lightnings, and an earthquake." When that happened there appeared seven angels prepared to sound their seven trumpets. Each trumpet was to announce a different sorrow or harsh punishment to the beast and his believers.

It's important here to pause and understand the extent of this damage and carnage. Many readers, especially the many devout Christians in America, understand these actions to be against everyone in the world, especially Americans. Why against America? Because so many have falsely interpreted that the 'evil Babylon' described in Chapter 17, Verse 5, refers to the actions and events taking place in America since we have been turned to a nation of 'evil and ungodly sinners.'

As I have already explained in previous chapters, and many writings before that, the Babylon described in Revelation, Chapter 17, is that of Islam. Islam is that beast, that Mother of Harlots. In truth, the United States, America, is the last great bastion to defend Israel and God's Commandments. Our nation was founded on those Christian principles; and there will be many martyrs in his name during this time of great tribulation to prove America's deep love and devotion to his Word. Our greatest challenge at this time is to survive the danger from that false prophet among us who attempts to destroy our Christian foundation and replace it with that great Islamic beast. You know his name. Revelation clearly describes him as a blasphemer and a deceiver.

Raise your head Americans and other citizens of the Word; do not be deceived by these lies and blasphemies of Satan's angels. As I write this book, one of Satan's great angels lives among us and leads our nation from the highest position. To avoid that poison spewing forth from his mouth we must hold fast, as admonished in John's letters to the Seven Churches; 'Hold fast.' Those words from Christ were meant for us as much as for those of the Seven Churches.

Although we will suffer through many days of tribulation, at least three and a half years, the seven angels will blow their trumpets to announce the more extreme horrors brought upon Babylon's children, primarily in the great Muslim nations of the Middle East. Verse 7 announces the trumpet of the first angel:

"The first angel sounded, and there followed hail and fire mingled with blood, and they were cast upon the earth; and the third part of trees was burnt up, and all green grass was burnt up."

Certainly, this must represent a nuclear event. Hail, fire and blood would be a combination of the return to earth from a nuclear explosion that rose heavenly with that high-rising mushroom cloud after the bomb had been dropped in or near the vicinity of many people. This likely would be a local event, where trees and grass were incinerated as the earth under and near the explosion was affected. Since this was initiated by the angels who stood before God, that would suggest the followers of the beast were the ones receiving this horrible death blow.

Verse 8 explains what happened when the second angel sounded, "And the second angel sounded, and as it were a great mountain burning with fire was cast into the sea: and the third part of the sea became blood."

Now, at this point it's almost instinctive to imagine the mountain moved into a body of water, a sea. Here, that's not the case. Recalling an earlier explanation; sea ordinarily means a 'sea of humanity - people.' Again, it must be remembered that John was describing things he saw from a vision; not things that were explained to him by Christ. This is what John saw but at that time had no way to describe in modern current terms. The words did not exist to explain exactly what he saw. He couldn't say he saw a giant mushroom cloud, the size of a mountain, move over a group of many people, and they were left dead and bloody. Verse 9 continues the vision:

"And the third part of the creatures which were in the sea, and had life, died; and the third part of the ships were destroyed."

This verse likely describes an actual water event, since it mentions creatures of the sea and ships. Certainly, any attack upon a nation, or a larger consortium, would include destruction of the infrastructure and support facilities. In all wars throughout history, the source of providing military support; such as rail lines, highways, and factories, has always been one of the first and primary targets against the enemy. The same would surely apply here.

What's the greatest support system of funding, militarily and otherwise, for those great Muslim nations? Oil. How is most of their oil transported? By ships. Therefore, their ships would be one of the first targets of a major attack. Ships would be destroyed, along with the other creatures of the sea surrounding that attack; likely another nuclear attack to destroy that many ships with that much collateral destruction. Destruction of that infrastructure will be the primary cause of tribulation throughout the rest of the world. Oil distribution would suddenly be disrupted; complicating availability and distribution of that major power source throughout the world. Further, the spilling of all that oil would 'turn the waters to blood.'

The introduction of the third angel, in Verse 10, sounding the third trumpet reveals a different and surprising star: "And the third angel sounded, and there fell a great star from heaven, burning as it were a lamp, and it fell upon the third part of the rivers, and upon the fountains of waters;11) And the name of the star is called Wormwood: and the third part of the waters became wormwood; and many men died of the waters, because they were made bitter."

Again, this is not a giant gaseous star falling from heaven. Instead this is simply the method of saying 'this is something important.' It represents a major event. This verse even calls it a 'great' star. It's that important. But, if it's not an actual physical galactic star, then what does it mean?

Almost daily for the past four years I've been trying to interpret different parts of Revelation. This part that mentioned wormwood had me totally lost without a single clue. Suddenly, a clue came out of nowhere.

My answer came from a very unusual place. Having a hurt knee, I was watching television waiting for it to heal and happened upon one of my favorite programs, 'The Artful Detective' which is a cute little show on Ovation. The shy detective, Murdoch, was on his first date with the lady doctor, Dr. Ogden, who performs their post-mortems; it was a picnic. To help overcome their shyness, they were drinking absinthe, which they also called the 'green fairy.' During their babble,

Murdoch mentioned wormwood. Wow - did my ears perk up and I immediately headed to google. In my research I learned that wormwood is a common plant with several varieties. The plants are used for making absinthe, an alcoholic drink; and another surprise - also for making synthetic cannabis. This is the information about wormwood offered by Wikipedia:

"Artemisia absinthium (absinthium, absinthe wormwood, wormwood, common wormwood, green ginger or grand wormwood) is a species of Artemisia, native to temperate regions of Eurasia and Northern Africa and widely naturalized in Canada and the northern United States. It is grown as an ornamental plant and is used as an ingredient in the spirit absinthe as well as some other alcoholic drinks.

Artemisia absinthium is a herbaceous, perennial plant with fibrous roots. The stems are straight, growing to 0.8–1.2 metres (2 ft 7 in–3 ft 11 in) (rarely 1.5 m, but, sometimes even larger) tall, grooved, branched, and silvery-green. The leaves are spirally arranged, greenish-grey above and white below, covered with silky silvery-white trichomes, and bearing minute oil-producing glands; the basal leaves are up to 25 cm long, bipinnate to tripinnate with long petioles, with the cauline leaves (those on the stem) smaller, 5–10 cm long, less divided, and with short petioles; the uppermost leaves can be both simple and sessile (without a petiole). Its flowers are pale yellow, tubular, and clustered in spherical bent-down heads (capitula), which are in turn clustered in leafy and branched panicles. Flowering is from early summer to early autumn; pollination is anemophilous. The fruit is a small achene; seed dispersal is by gravity. It grows naturally on uncultivated, arid ground, on rocky slopes, and at the edge of footpaths and fields."

The plants are used for making absinthe, an alcoholic drink. And there's another great surprise. It's also for making synthetic cannabis. With this information about wormwood, we can now interpret the meaning of verse 10, 'upon the third part of the rivers, and upon the fountains of waters.' The rivers refer to the flow of humanity; the fountains of waters refer to young people from which those rivers flow.

At this point, I could go into a large explanation about the problems of addiction to alcohol, marijuana, heroin, and other addictive opiates; but I won't. All people are aware of this problem, and in too many cases have relatives addicted to these substances. To describe everything would consume the remainder of the pages of this book; that's not the purpose for this book. But, one might safely say that a third part of mankind is affected by this problem created by that great star; Wormwood. Next, verse 12 introduces the fourth angel:

"And the fourth angel sounded, and the third part of the sun was smitten, and the third part of the moon, and the third part of the stars; so as the third part of them was darkened, and the day shone not for a third part of it, and the night likewise." This seems to say that the sky and heavens were darkened from all the war activity. It could mean smoke and sulphur from artillery shells and bombs; but most likely it's the result from nuclear clouds in that battle region. Then the next verse, 13, says to prepare for what's to come; it will be worse.

"And I beheld, and heard an angel flying through the midst of heaven, saying with a loud voice, Woe, woe, woe, to the inhabiters of the earth by reason of the other voices of the trumpet of the three angels, which are yet to sound!" Then Chapter 9 introduces the fifth angel:

"And the fifth angel sounded, and I saw a star fall from heaven unto the earth: and to him was given the key to the bottomless pit. 2) And he opened the bottomless pit; and there arose a smoke out of the pit, as the smoke of a great furnace; and the sun and air were darkened by reason of the smoke of the pit. 3) And there came out of the smoke locusts upon the earth; and unto them was given power, as the scorpions of the earth have power." This is considered the first of the three woes.

Verses 3 through 6 describe the purpose of the locusts that rose in the smoke of the bottomless pit. That purpose was not to hurt any green thing or a tree, but to hurt only those men who do not have the seal of God in their forehead; those who worship God. And, they were not to kill those men, but only to torment them for five months. That torment will be so severe that men will desire to die but, "death shall flee from them." The next verses, 7 through 10 describe those locusts which provided that torment:

They were shaped like horses prepared for battle; their crowns were as of gold, and their faces were like the faces of men. They also had hair like women, teeth like lions, and breastplates of iron. Verse 9 offers the best clue of their identity: "...and the sound of their wings was as the sound of chariots of many horses running into battle." Verse 10 continues: "And they had tails like unto scorpions, and there were stings in their tails: and their power was to hurt men five months." 11) And they had a king over them, which is the angel of the bottomless pit, whose name in the Hebrew is Abaddon, but in the Greek tongue his name Apollyon." So, what could all this information mean; it's so coded? There are three code words that explain what John saw.

First, there were so many they looked like locusts forming on the horizon. As they got closer, John could see they looked like scorpions; their tales were like the stinger part of a scorpion. Second, the 'sound of their wings' certainly confirms they were aerial vehicles; helicopters, if they were shaped like a scorpion. Third, the two words, Abaddon and Apollyon, refer to or suggest 'a destroyer.' Therefore, the most likely interpretation of this event is that helicopters were used against the beast's resources to destroy his base; to hurt them, not to kill the men.

Verse 12 reads: "One woe is past; and behold, there come two woes more, hereafter." Then after a message from heaven telling the sixth angel with the trumpet to loose the four angels which are bound in the great river Euphrates, those four angels were loosed. Then Verse 15 adds: "And the four angels were loosed, which were prepared for an hour, and a day, and a month, and a year, for to slay the third part of men."

Now this also is often misinterpreted as a third of all men on earth. Taken in perspective of the other events, this rationally would mean a third of those in that battle. This also suggests the battle will last a little more than thirteen months. Verse 16 gives the number of fighters, "And the number of the army of the horsemen were two hundred thousand thousand; and I heard the number of them."

This suggests several things. First, an armed force from four nations had been preparing near the Euphrates River to invade a large area held by forces led by evil. It's not stated or even suggested if this is an international force or a force of other Muslims that would go forth to 'kill one another' as revealed in Revelation 6:4. Another applicable reference is in Chapter 17, which describes the beast, Islam, in full. Verse 16 states the beast will hate the 'whore' part of the beast, "and shall make her desolate and naked, and shall eat her flesh and burn her with fire." The next verse adds: "For God hath put in their hearts to fulfill his will."

Verse 17 describes the fighting force attacking that evil: "And I saw the horses in the vision, and them that sat on them, having breastplates of fire, and of jacinth, and brimstone: and the heads of the horses were as the heads of lions; and out of their mouths issued fire and smoke and brimstone." Again, John didn't have the nouns, the words, to describe what he saw in current-day descriptions. In those days, warriors rode horses or chariots. Today, they would be described as tanks and other armored vehicles; that can fire shells, fire, and other propellants.

Can you imagine trying to describe the actions and results of a fully armed tank two thousand years ago. John did the best he could in the fewest number of words. Would it have sounded better if he had said, "I saw these big metal things, bigger than elephants, coming over the horizon; and something was coming out of their mouths. It was fire with some other things with that fire. I don't know exactly what they were. And, the sun glistening on them made them appear as jacinth and brimstone; and then continuing in that ramble? Of course not. The readers of his time would have asked, 'But, where are the horses and chariots?'

Verse 18 adds, "By these three was the third part of men killed, by the fire, and by the smoke, and by the brimstone, which issued out of their mouths." Verse 19 adds as a summary, "For their power is in their mouth, and in their tails: for their tails were like unto serpents, and had heads, and with them they do hurt." After all this horror and woe, did they capitulate; repent? The next two verses answer this question:

"And the rest of the men which were not killed by these plagues yet repented not of the works of their hands, that they should not worship devils, and idols of gold, and silver, and brass, and stone, and of wood: which neither can see, nor hear, nor walk: Neither repented they of their murders, nor of their sorceries, nor of their fornication, nor of their thefts."

This sums up a description of Islam very well. They worship toward a wooden building in Mecca that houses a black satellite stone. Neither of these can see, hear, or walk. Plus, that religion if full of fornications such as having many wives, even below the age of nine. And they even consummate these abominable weddings; by raping little girls. And for their thefts: they rob and plunder every land they invade and conquer. Through peace, they destroy many. As for worshiping devils: Satan, the beast, and the false prophet are described together throughout Revelation. Satan leads them.

Chapter 10 takes a pause from the action to describe the effects of a 'little book.' The information is confusing because the verses infer that John is talking to two different angels and voices. In Verse 2, he described an angel that came down from heaven, "And he had in his hand a little book open: and he set his right foot upon the sea and his left foot on the earth." The description of this angel sounds like an angel from God, but his actions suggest otherwise. The description of this angel continues:

"And cried with a loud voice, as when a lion roareth: and when he cried, seven thunders uttered their voices." It continues in Verse 4: "And when the seven thunders had uttered their voices, I was about to write: and I heard a voice from heaven saying unto me, Seal up those things which the seven thunders uttered, and write them not."

In the next verses, that angel that had come down from heaven lifted his hand to heaven, "And sware by him that liveth for ever and ever, who created heaven, and the things that therein are, and the earth, and the things that therein are, and the earth, and the things that therein are, and the sea, and the things which are therein, that there should be time no longer." This 'there should be time no longer' seems to suggest an end of the world; but with a different interpretation than what seems obvious, that's not what it means. Let's consider several things that propose a different interpretation.

This 'mighty angel' that came down from heaven is not presented as a 'great' angel. This description is different. And, 'he cried as a lion roareth' describes a beast introduced in Chapter 13, Verse 2. It's the beast that rose up out of the sea as John stood on the sand of the sea. It's also the beast that had the 'mouth of a lion' given great power, and his power, and his seat, and great authority, by the dragon. This dragon, with his angels, is described again in 12:7-9:

"And there was war in heaven: Michael and his angels fought against the dragon; and the dragon fought and his angels, And prevailed not;

neither was their place found any more in heaven. And the great dragon was cast out, that old serpent, called the Devil, and Satan, which deceiveth the whole world: he was cast out into the earth, and his angels were cast out with him."

The likely interpretation of this scene is that Satan, that mighty angel, came down from heaven; with a little book in his hand. That book represented the changes he planned when he thought he would replace God; 'that there should be time no longer' of God's work. If that's the case, then what did that 'little book' represent? That answer now becomes very clear; assuming Satan had planned to replace God; which he tries to do every day. So, what is that 'little book?' It's the book Muslims now call their Holy Koran. Now that we know what it probably is, let's listen to what John said he did with it. But first, Verse 7 sets the stage:

"But in the days of the voice of the seventh angel, when he shall begin to sound, the mystery of God should be finished, as he hath declared to his servants the prophets." In other words, when this new challenge arises, there should be no doubt to his people and the world who he really is. This challenge will make him more real. John continues in Verse 8:

"And the voice which I heard from heaven spake unto me again, and said, Go and take the little book which is open in the hand of the angel which standeth upon the sea and upon the earth, 9) And I went unto the angel, and said unto him, Give me the little book. And he (the voice from heaven, not the one holding the little book) said unto me, Take it, and eat it up; and it shall make they belly bitter, but it shall be in thy mouth sweet as honey. 10) And I took the little book out of the angel's hand, and ate it up; and it was in my mouth sweet as honey; and as soon as I had eaten it, my belly was bitter. 11) And he (the voice from heaven) said unto me, Thou must prophesy again before many peoples, and nations, and tongues, and kings."

139

That 'sweet taste' in John's mouth is similar to his first impression in another chapter. Chapter 17 describes the rise of that beast, Islam. That experience begins in Verse 6: "And I saw the woman drunken with the blood of the saints and with the blood of the martyrs of Jesus: and when I saw her, I wondered with great admiration. 7) And the angel said unto me, Wherefore didst thou marvel?"

What do these two events mean? It means the beast, Islam, will offer many ideas and concepts that sound wonderful and inviting which are deceptions to replace God; 'that there should be time no longer.' These deceptions offer peace and a wonderful hereafter if one follows that false god; but in reality the result is death and having one's name stricken from the 'book of life.'

That great appeal, at which John marveled and that was in the mouth as sweet as honey, is the danger revealed to John. It's the reason the voice from heaven told John, "Thou must prophesy again before many peoples, and nations, and tongues, and kings." This warning is the reason and the purpose for the Book of Revelation. John's writing of the Book of Revelation is that prophesy given to 'many peoples, and nations, and tongues, and kings.' Revelation is a warning not to be swayed away from God's Word by the promise of 'sweet' things. Chapter 10 is relatively short, but it reveals much.

Chapter 11 reveals who will stand against the beast as prophets. It begins with the instruction to measure a temple and an alter with 'a reed like unto a rod.' But, perhaps this measurement is not for a physical place, but instead for foundations of God and Christ; since the next verses, 3-4, read, "And I will give power unto my two witnesses, and they shall prophesy a thousand two hundred and threescore days, clothed in sackcloth. These are the two olive trees and the two candlesticks standing before the God of the earth."

(Catherine Emmerich revealed that Enoch and Elias are in Paradise where they await their return to the world to preach at the End of

Time. It's her vision that these will be the two prophets 'clothed in sackcloth.')

Olive trees are customarily accepted as a sign of peace; and candlesticks were explained in the beginning of Revelation as churches. Therefore, it would be logical to accept that God was speaking to His two churches that offer peace and salvation: Jewish and Christian. The next few verses explain what happens to these two prophets. After they are protected for three and a half years, having great authority, they will be killed by the beast from the bottomless pit, who shall, "make war against them, and shall overcome them and kill them." The prophesy continues:

Their bodies will lie in the streets for three and a half days, unburied, while, 10) "And they that dwell upon the earth shall rejoice over them, and make merry, and shall send gifts one to another; because these two prophets tormented them that dwell on the earth." After that three and a half days, God's Spirit of life entered into them, and they stood on their feet. When that happened those watching became very fearful. As they watched those ascend up to heaven in a cloud, 13) And the same hour was there a great earthquake and the tenth part of the city fell, and in the earthquake were slain men of seven thousand: and the remnant were affraighted, and gave glory to the God of heaven. 14) The second woe is past; and, behold, the third woe cometh quickly."

Verse 15, "And the seventh angel sounded; and there were great voices in heaven, saying, The kingdoms of this world are become the kingdoms of our Lord, and of his Christ; and he shall reign for ever and ever. Then Verses 18 and 19 show the conclusion of that wrath, that third woe:

And the nations were angry, and thy wrath is come, and the time of the dead, that they should be judged, and that thou shouldest give reward unto thy servants the prophets, and to the saints, and them that fear thy name, small and great; and shouldest destroy them which destroy the earth. And the temple of God was opened in heaven, and there was seen in his temple the ark of this testament; and there were lightnings, and voices, and thunderings, and an earthquake, and great hail."

This indicates the final battle to destroy the beast, that destroyer, had begun. Great hail suggests many rockets and missiles, and perhaps nuclear weapons, will be used against the beast in his own land, and even perhaps Israel; that had been occupied for that three and a half years of the tribulation. This was the final of the three woes against the beast.

Chapter 9
The Countdown

C hapters 12 and 13 have already been discussed, in parts. Chapter 12 describes the birth of Christ and the rise of Christianity. It concludes that the dragon continues to war against the woman, Christianity: "And the dragon was wroth with the woman, and went to make war with the remnant of her seed, which keep the commandments of God, and have the testimony of Jesus Christ."

Chapter 13 describes the rise of the first beast, known otherwise as the antichrist, from the sea of humanity; which introduces Muhammad. At his death, Verse 10: "He that killeth with the sword must be killed with the sword," then rises the second beast. The second beast is also known as the false prophet. The second beast is the one who creates the 'mark of the beast.' His plans and actions are more subtle and deceitful than those of the first beast. He causes things to happen; he doesn't necessarily make things happen.

That final countdown preview begins in Chapter 14 and continues through Chapter 16. There it pauses in Chapter 17, where an angel holding one of the seven vials explains the rise of Islam, who is identified as 'The Mother of Harlots.' In that explanation, it's revealed that Islam, that nation, is also the one known as current-day Babylon. After all these participants are revealed and identified, then Chapter 14 announces the beginning of the battle situations. It begins:

"And I looked, and, lo, a Lamb stood on the mount Si'on, and with him an hundred forty and four thousand, having his Father's name written in their foreheads." Then Verse 4 describes them as those, "who were not defiled with women; for they are virgins. These are they which follow the Lamb withersoever he goeth. These were redeemed from among men, being the first-fruits unto God and to the Lamb."

Obviously, these 144,000 are the same as those who converted from Jewish to Christian in an earlier verse. This verse says they had worshiped neither woman, Christian or Islam; they were virgins, until they converted to Christianity; to follow Christ. Then, they were redeemed to God and to Christ, and had not been influenced by Islam.

The next few verses describe three angels coming forth to issue warnings. The first angel flew in the midst of heaven, "having the everlasting gospel to preach unto them that dwell on the earth and to every nation, and kindred and tongue, and people, 7) Saying with a loud voice, Fear God, and give glory to him for the hour of his judgment is come: and worship him that made heaven, and earth, and the sea, and the fountains of waters."

The second angel followed, announcing that Babylon has fallen, that great city, because, "she made all nations drink of the wine of the wrath of her fornication." Then there was a third angel saying that if any man were to worship the beast and his image, and accept his mark, 10) "The same shall drink of the wine of the wrath of God...and he shall be tormented with fire and brimstone in the presence of the holy angels, and in the presence of the Lamb."

These three angels gave a stern warning to that beast's followers that horrible things were about to happen if they didn't turn from their worship of that beast, Satan, and repent of their acceptance of him by their mark. That was the stern warnings for those blasphemers to repent. Then John heard a voice from heaven telling him to write to his followers who would suffer from the upcoming battle. Verse 13 gives that encouragement: "And I heard the voice from heaven saying unto me, Write, Blessed are the dead which die in the Lord from henceforth: Yea, saith the Spirit, that they may rest from their labours; and their works do follow them." The next verses describe the battle preparation by both sides. It's the gathering of their forces.

Verses 14-16 describe how Christ's forces were chosen first. "And I looked, and behold a white cloud, and upon the cloud one sat like unto the Son of man, having on his head a golden crown, and in his hand a sharp sickle." Then another angel appeared and told him to thrust in his sickle and reap (meaning to gather his forces) "for the harvest of the earth is ripe." Then he thrust in his sickle and the earth was reaped.

Verses 17-19 describe Satan's preparation. "And another angel came out of the temple which is in heaven, he also having a sharp sickle." Then another angel 'who had power over fire' said to him to cast in his sickle and reap, "Thrust in they sharp sickle, and gather the clusters of the vine of the earth; for her grapes are fully ripe. And the angel thrust in his sickle into the earth, and gathered the vine of the earth, and cast it into the great winepress of the wrath of God." Then verse 20 shows the results when they met:

"And the winepress was trodden without the city, and blood came out of the winepress, even unto the horse bridles, by the space of a thousand and six hundred furlongs."

Chapter 15 considers the jubilation of the great victory then offers praises to the power and strength of God in Verse 4: "Who shall not fear thee, O Lord, and glorify thy name? For thou only art holy: for all nations shall come and worship before thee; for they judgments are made manifest." This is a proclamation that the other who claims to be holy is not, and that eventually his followers will depart him and come to worship God; "for all nations shall come and worship before thee."

The next verses reveal a new door was open in heaven from which seven angels emerged. Then they were given seven vials full of the wrath of God, to be dispersed unto the followers of the beast. Verse 8 explains the followers of the beast would not be accepted into his Word until all the vials had been emptied:

"And the temple was filled with smoke from the glory of God, and from his power; and no man was able to enter into the temple, till the seven plagues of the seven angels were fulfilled."

Then Chapter 16 begins: "And I heard a great voice out of the temple saying to the seven angels, Go your ways, and pour out the vials of the wrath of God upon the earth. 2) And the first went, and poured out his vial upon the earth; and there fell a noisome and grievous sore upon the men which had the mark of the beast, and upon them which worshiped his image."

This most likely scene is explained from that earlier nuclear event. Those nearby who were not killed instantly from the nuclear blast would certainly have suffered from thermal and radiation burns. These would cause those sores upon those men. According to the earlier verse, even if they were inclined to repent and accept the Word of God, they would still have to wait until all seven vials had been poured out before they would be accepted into that temple.

Results from the second vial are more cryptic. "And the second angel poured out his vial upon the sea; and it became as the blood of a dead man; and every living soul died in the sea." Contents of the third vial poured upon 'the rivers and fountains of waters' could have created the same results; the waters were contaminated which made them distasteful and undrinkable. From an earthly and realistic standpoint, how could this happen?

It's easy to visualize that when bombs and other artillery fire, including nuclear bombs, were dropped on those areas, certainly their drinking waters, ponds, rivers, bays, and nearby larger bodies of water would also become contaminated; and undrinkable. And, in some cases the oil wells and oil distribution infrastructure would also be destroyed; leaving that oil to flow freely into those water systems. Also, as the debris, oil, and blood returned to earth as the mushroom cloud eroded it could cover a broad area of water, and would have the appearance of blood.

It's also certain, in some cases, that oil would be mixed with mud and clay and would appear as blood when it flowed into the waters. In summary, their waters would look like blood and would be undrinkable. Verse 6 summarizes with a conclusion of justification for those acts: "For they have shed the blood of saints and prophets, and thou hast given them blood to drink; for they are worthy." In other words, they deserve nothing better than blood to drink. Their evil makes them unworthy of good clean water.

Verse 8 continues with the fourth vial: "And the fourth angel poured out his vial upon the sun; and power was given unto him to scorch men with fire." This most likely referred to the great heat of the nuclear activity. Those under or near the explosions would be instantly incinerated, while those further away would feel the great heat. Verse 9 says even that great event didn't change their evil, "...and they repented not to give him glory."

Results of the fifth vial were explained in Verse 10, "And the fifth angel poured out his vial upon the seat of the beast; and his kingdom was full of darkness; and they gnawed their tongues for pain." This doesn't detail the location of the 'seat' of the beast, but most certainly it would be in the Muslim strongholds, where much oil is produced. Any warfare in that location would result in much dust and darkness. The next verse, 11, states their stubborn resistance to relent: "And blasphemed the God of heaven because of their pains and their sores, and repented not of their deeds."

Verse 12 details the results of the sixth vial. It was poured upon the great river Euphrates, causing it to dry up, "...that the way of the kings of the east might be prepared." Obviously, the Euphrates River had to be crossed for the large armies to invade; likely into Israel and its surrounding territory. In modern terms this drying up to cross can be accomplished with bridges; which is more likely to happen than the river actually drying up.

Then Verses 13 and 14 change from reporting physical events to persuasions and motivations. It describes how the spirits of Satan, the beast, and the false prophet go forth to convince and prepare the evil ones for war, "For they are the spirits of devils, working miracles, which go forth unto the kings of the earth and of the whole world, to gather them to the battle of that great day of God Almighty."

Verse 15 is a direct message from God. It says He will come as a thief; to pay attention and be prepared for that day. Then the next verse says God gathered them together in a place the Hebrews call Armageddon. This is a likely reference to the large Jezreel Valley which is overlooked by Tell Megiddo, near Mount Zion. This is the location of many historical battles.

Then verse 17 begins the explanation of what happened when the seventh vial was poured into the air. "And there came a great voice out of the temple of heaven, from the throne, saying, It is done." And, that's when all hell breaks loose.

Verse 18: "And there were voices, and thunders, and lightenings; and there was a great earthquake, such as was not since men were upon the earth, so mighty an earthquake, and so great." Verse 21: "And there fell upon men a great hail out of heaven, every stone about the weight of a talent: and men blasphemed God because of the plague of the hail; for the plague thereof was exceeding great." Although the talent had different weights from different areas and times, research suggests the talent at this time was about 130 pounds. No other information is given about this hail, but one likelihood is that it was projectiles fired from ships or other large artillery. This weight would be too heavy for other armaments such as mortars. Many of them falling out of the sky at the same time, seen by someone who had never heard of firepower and projectiles other than arrows, might be considered 'great hail.' How else could they have been described?

Then Chapter 17 digresses to explain what had happened. One of the seven angels invites John to accompany him into the 'Spirit of the wilderness' where he can see. This is where John is shown the woman riding the scarlet-colored beast, full of names of blasphemy, having seven heads and ten horns.

In Verses 5 and 6 the angel describes the woman, Mystery Babylon, "drunken with the blood of the saints and with the blood of the martyrs of Jesus." Clearly, the war has been against that religion called Islam. That chapter explains further that Islam is in two parts; one part identified as the whore will be attacked by the beast, having the seven heads and ten horns.

Verses 7 through 12 describe the beast in a very coded message, "The beast that thou sawest was, and is not; and shall ascend out of the bottomless pit, and go into perdition (ruin and destruction:) and they that dwell on the earth shall wonder, whose names were not written in the book of life from the foundation of the world, when they behold the beast that was, and is not, and yet is." Verse 11 seems the key, "And the beast that was, and is not, even he is the eighth, and is of the seven, and goeth into perdition."

Perhaps this is referring to the spirit of Muhammad, who was assumed to be killed on the battlefield at Uhud, but who rose again. Perhaps his spirit arose to become one of the eight; those eight are still to be determined, and time will soon show who they are.

Then Verse 13 summarizes, "These have one mind, (those that dwell on the earth shall wonder, whose names were not written in the book of life from the foundation of the world) and shall give their power and strength unto the beast." That beast referring to the mother religion; Islam. Verse 14 explains what happens to them when they make war with Christ: "...and the Lamb shall overcome them: for he is Lord of lords, and King of kings: and they that are with him are called and chosen, and faithful." Verses 16 and 17 are the actions that describe the rider of the red horse 'that they should kill one another.'

"And the ten horns which thou sawest upon the beast, shall hate the whore, and shall make her desolate and naked, and shall eat her flesh, and burn her with fire. For God hath put in their hearts to fulfill his will, and to agree, and give their kingdom unto the beast, until the words of God shall be fulfilled. This also fulfills his promise referring to that woman, Jezebel, 2:23, to "kill her children with death."

Chapter 18 is a summary of more details in a later chapter, but part of that summary is pertinent in this chapter describing the rider of the black horse in Chapter 6. I could summarize the following information, but I think it's critical to expose the exact words as written in the Bible. There's also a warning to 'take not from the words.' These words are critical to understanding that woman, Babylon.

This chapter begins with John writing more: "And after these things I saw another angel come down from heaven, having great power and the earth was lightened with his glory. And he cried mightily with a strong voice, saying, Babylon the great is fallen, is fallen, and is become the habitation of devils, and the hold of every foul spirit, and a cage of every unclean and hateful bird." Verse 3 repeats an earlier comment about that woman:

"For all nations have drunk of the wine of the wrath of her

fornication, and the kings of the earth have committed fornication with her, and the merchants of the earth are waxed rich through the abundance of her delicacies."

The following reference, Verses 4 and 5, is perhaps the most important admonition in the book of Revelation. Revelation is a warning - the purpose for the Book. It epitomizes the warnings given to the seven churches; 'those who have an ear, pay attention to what will happen in the future.'

Verse 4: "And I heard another voice from heaven, saying, come out of her, my people, that ye be not partakers of her sins, and that ye receive not of her plagues. Verse 5: "For her sins have reached unto heaven, and God hath remembered her inequities."

This warning is very clear. We have a choice: become part of that city of Babylon by becoming a Muslim or by respecting that religion,' or turn away and refuse to accept any part of its abomination. (For example: when an adult man marries a nine-year-old girl; is that not an abomination? This is only one of Islam's abominations in the eyes of the Lord, or any respectable human being. And, if we accept that abomination we are thus respecting that Babylon.) Verse 6 is the firm warning to that religion - that woman:

"Reward her even as she rewarded you, and double unto her double according to her works; in the cup which she hath filled fill to her double." Verse 10 indicates the judgement against the woman: "Standing afar off for the fear of her torment, saying, Alas, alas that great city Babylon, that mighty city! For in one hour is thy judgement come."

Verse 11 shows the beginning and the results of that destruction of Babylon from the wrath of God. This includes the lack of merchandise and other necessities of commerce (mankind things- the beast with the face of a man that introduced the rider of the black horse) that have made many rich and wealthy:

"And the merchants of the earth shall weep and mourn over her; for no man buyeth their merchandise any more: 12, The merchandise of gold, and silver, and precious stone, and of pearls, and fine linen, and purple, and silk and scarlet, and all thyine wood, and all manner of vessels of ivory, and all manner of vessels of most precious wood, and of brass, and iron, and marble."

Verse 13 continues to itemize that list; but with one strange difference; the last item in this list, "And cinnamon, and odours, and ointments, and frankincense, and wine, and oil, and fine flour, and wheat, and beasts, and sheep, and horses, and chariots, and slaves, and souls of men." In this list, souls of men seem to be placed as an afterthought. In effect, however, it's placed last in this list to suggest that this commercial process drew men's souls into the religion for the purposes of participation; and for having access to their major commodity - oil. Verse 15 summarizes the results of the lack of commerce:

"The merchants of these things, which were made rich by her, shall stand afar off for the fear of her torment, weeping and wailing." Now, how do we know this is the same woman drunken with the blood of the saints described in Chapter 17, Verse 6? The paragraph above states two colors out of context: purple and scarlet. Verse 4 in that chapter describes the woman as 'arrayed in purple and scarlet color.'

Chapter 18 continues that long list of items that are no longer available through commerce to make men rich anymore. After that long list of non-available items their agony is repeated in Verses 15-17:

"The merchants of these things, which were made rich by her, shall stand afar off for the fear of torment, weeping and wailing, And saying, Alas, alas that great city, that was clothed in fine linen, and purple and scarlet, and decked with gold, and precious stones, and pearls! For in one hour so great riches is come to nought. And every shipmaster, and all the company in ships, and sailors, and as many as trade by sea, stood afar off. 18) And cried when they saw the smoke of her burning, saying, What city is like unto this great city! So what is the clue that the major item of commerce, the one that made many men of ships rich? The answer: the colors of scarlet and purple.

Again, 'her' and 'scarlet' are connected. Also, why are the colors scarlet and purple mentioned two times in those lists? Because purple and scarlet (red) are colors of amber; the natural color of oil. Simply, when those men made rich from using oil in their commerce, they suffered agony; 'weeping and wailing.'

Then Verse 24 suggests a feeling of relief by the apostles and prophets who had toiled at victory over the beast. "Rejoice over her, thou heaven, and ye holy apostles and prophets; for God hath avenged you on her." This was likely in answer to those in 6:10, as their souls waited under that alter, asking, "And they cried with a loud voice, saying, How long, O Lord, holy and true, dost thou not judge and avenge our blood on them that dwell on the earth?"

Chapter 18 concludes with Verse 24, which gives the final view of that defeated woman: "And in her was found the blood of prophets, and of saints, and of all that were slain upon the earth."

Chapter 10
The Last Battle

A n important question at this point is; how was that great 'battle of Armageddon' in the Middle East, specifically in Israel, allowed to occur? Certainly with the great power and influence of the United States in world events, that war should not have happened. Moral suasion, if not actual threats and show of force, should have prevented it. How can small nations be allowed to create such havoc and horror on the world stage? Perhaps 2 Thessalonians 2:7 answers this question:

"And now ye know what withholdeth that he might be revealed in his time. For the mystery of iniquity doth already work; only he who now letteth will let, until he be taken out of the way." This pertains to protecting Israel from an Islamic attack, especially from Iran.

Historically, the United States has pledged to offer protection to Israel - an attack against Israel is an attack against the United States. Today, under the current presidential administration there is little concern being expressed to carry out that caveat. The current administration seems more devoted to 'the woman arrayed in purple and scarlet' than to Israel; that Israel that forms the basis of our Judeo-Christian religion.

Secondly, Iran is determined to invade Israel - especially with a nuclear weapon. Their determination is guided by their belief in a 'Mahdi' who is waiting in occultation (hiding on the sidelines?) for a major catastrophe so he can reveal himself and rid the world of infidels so the only people left alive on earth are Muslims. In copying the Christian religion, this is their Messiah (taking the place of the return of Christ) that will save the world. Only in this case it's to kill all the other non-believers so it can be a 'pure' world for Islam. Seriously.

For this belief, they must attack Israel to create this holocaustic event. On the other hand we must also consider the possibility that only a few evil and personal power-driven leaders of those nations, especially Iran, are determined to create a world leadership position for themselves - and it has nothing to do with religion or a false religion; it could be based on a pure personal power driven motive.

Throughout history, that has not been an unusual motive. And sadly, in this case as in cases throughout history, normal citizens have no choice but to follow and support that power-crazed leader; or they will be killed. Recent perfect examples are Adolph Hitler, Joseph Stalin, Benito Mussolini, and Mao Tse Tung. If Iran were to succeed in its conquest, we would soon be filled with the name of their great leader. That drive for personal power always results in the death of many innocents; against their will. Chapter 19 seems somewhat confusing in that it suggests another battle.

Chapter 19 is simply a recapitulation of the war that had already taken place. It begins, "And after these things I heard a great voice of much people in heaven saying, Alleluia; Salvation; Salvation, and glory, and honor, and power, unto the Lord our God;"(Glory, honor, and power are three of the seven spirits of God.)

Verse 2 continues, "For true and righteous are his judgements ; for he hath judged the great whore, which did corrupt the earth with her fornication, and hath avenged the blood of his servants at her hand." Then Verse 6 takes a new turn that suggests a combining of 'many waters.' Verse 7 also contains a coded suggestion.

"And I heard as it were the voice of a great multitude, and as the voice of many waters, and as the voice of mighty thunderings, saying, Alleluia: for the Lord God omnipotent reigneth." 7) Let us be glad and rejoice, and give honour to him: for the marriage of the Lamb is come, and his wife hath made herself ready."

Before we continue exploring the information in Chapter 19, let's go forward into the last two chapters of Revelation and examine four verses that will add to the understanding of the next verses in Chapter 19. From Chapters 21 and 22, let's examine these four verses and consider a conclusion:

Verses 22-24: "And I saw no temple therein: for the Lord God Almighty and the Lamb are the temple of it. And the city had no need of the sun, neither of the moon, to shine in it: for the glory of God did lighten it, and the Lamb is the light thereof. And the nations of them which are saved shall walk in the light of it: and the kings of the earth do bring their glory and honour into it."

Verse 2 in Chapter 22: "In the midst of the street of it, (a pure river of water of life) and on either side of the river, was there the tree of life, which bare twelve manner of fruits, and yielded her fruit every month: and the leaves of the tree were for the healing of the nations."

The conclusions: These four verses suggest two things. First, there was only one temple in the great city, that New Jerusalem. It was the temple of God and Christ recognized as one: Jews now recognized the Messiah, and He and God were seen by both religions as one and the same; there was only one temple.

Second: the earth will not be destroyed after those great battles; life on earth will continue in an earthly form. This is taken from those two verses: "And the nations of them which are saved...and the leaves of the tree were for the healing of the nations." Certainly, these leaves mentioned are only as a metaphor; since many cultures in the past,

157

and some still today, use the application of special leaves for cures of many injuries and diseases. Now, let's return to Chapter 19.

Remember from Verse 6, "...for the Lord God omnipotent reigneth?" Then Verse 7 "...for the marriage of the Lamb is come and his wife hath made herself ready." From the information in Chapters 21 and 22, this certainly suggests that the two great religions that worship God will now both worship God and Christ; the one they will both recognize as omnipotent.

That recognition continues in Verse 9: "And he saith unto me, Write, Blessed are thy which are called unto the marriage supper of the lamb, And he saith unto me, These are the true sayings of God. 10) And I fell at his feet to worship him. And he said unto me, See thou do it not: I am thy fellowservant, and of thy brethren that have the testimony of Jesus: worship God: for the testimony of Jesus is the spirit of prophesy." Once combined as one religion that worships both Jesus and God, that last battle begins. Of course, that's the last battle before the end of the thousand years; often called the Millenium.

The next few verses seem a summary of things, but the question begins in verse 14 whether this is a summary or the vision of another battle. "And the armies which were in heaven followed him upon white horses, clothed in fine linen, white and clean." Verse 15 continues, "And out of his mouth goeth a sharp sword, that with it he should smite the nations; and he shall rule them with a rod of iron; and he treadeth the winepress of the fierceness and wrath of Almighty God." But, perhaps this is an indication that the Word of God goes forth to convert the wicked to Christianity with the 'sword of his mouth,' combined with an actual battle.

Several verses mention the two-edged sword of His mouth. Perhaps this means one edge if for the Word of God, and the other edge is the wrath of God fulfilled by those on earth who have the Spirits of God to do the actual battles.

Verse 17 begins the view of that last great battle: "And I saw an angel standing in the sun; and he cried with a loud voice, saying to all the fowls that fly in the midst of heaven, Come and gather yourselves together unto the supper of the great God; That ye may eat the flesh of kings, and the flesh of captains, and the flesh of mighty men, and the flesh of horses, and of them that sit on them, and the flesh of all men, both free and bond, both small and great." These were the bodies of those men described in 15:15-16 trying to hide in the dens and rocks of mountains. Verse 17 concluded for those: "For the great day of the wrath is come; and who shall be able to stand?"

Perhaps this was just a summary of the conclusion of the last battle, that battle of Armageddon, since it stated that the armies were gathered there. Verse 19 adds a similar reference and phrase:

"And I saw the beast, and the kings of the earth, and their armies, gathered together to make war against him that sat on the horse, and against his army." The next verses continue the event:

"And the beast was taken, and with him the false prophet that wrought miracles before him, with which he deceived them that had received the mark of the beast, and them that worshiped his image. These both were cast alive into a lake of fire burning with brimstone. 21, And the remnant were slain with the sword of him that sat upon the horse, which sword proceeded out of his mouth; and all the fowls were filled with their flesh."

Then, according to the next chapter God, "Laid hold on the dragon, that old serpent, which is the Devil and Satan, and bound him a thousand years, And cast him into the bottomless pit, and shut him up, and set a seal upon him, that he should deceive the nations no more, till the thousand years should be fulfilled."

Chapter 20 gives more details about events during that thousand years. It says that the souls of them that "were beheaded for the witness of Jesus and for the word of God and which had not worshiped the beast, neither his image, neither had received his mark upon their foreheads, or in their hands; and they lived and reigned with Christ a thousand years." This is the time known generally as the Millennium. This is also the time known as the first resurrection. The first resurrection includes only this sacrificing group. This is also the basis for another misconception of the Bible that concerns the rapture.

This event some speak of as the rapture does not exist. The first to be taken up to heaven to reign with Christ are the souls of those beheaded and sacrificed during this time of tribulation; and will reign with God that thousand years. No bodies of friends, family, and neighbors will suddenly be swept up in the clouds to disappear and reign with God during that thousand years. It's the souls of that special few. The souls of all others, dead and waiting under the alter, after that thousand years will be judged for resurrection based on the 'book of life.' These waiting souls are described in Chapter 6, when the fifth seal was opened. It includes verses 9 through 11:

"And when he had opened the fifth seal, I saw under the alter the souls of them that were slain for the word of God, and for the testimony which they held: And they cried with a loud voice, saying, How long, O Lord, holy and true, dost thou not judge and avenge our blood on them that dwell on the earth? And white robes were given unto every one of them; and it was said unto them, that they should rest yet for a little season, until their fellowservants also and their brethren, that they should be killed as they were, should be fulfilled."

Chapter 20 explains what happens to Satan after the thousand years when 'Satan shall be loosed out of his prison. And shall go out to deceive the nations which are in the four quarters of the earth, Gog and Magog, to gather them together to battle: the number of whom is as the sand of the sea.' That was Satan's biggest mistake because verse 9 tells his demise: "...and fire came down from God out of heaven and devoured them. 10, And the devil that deceived them was

160

cast into the lake of fire and brimstone, where the beast and the false prophet are, and shall be tormented day night for ever and ever." No other information is given about this last war with Satan. Good riddance.

Perhaps Gog and Magog might be determined during that thousand year period. There's nothing now to suggest what or who they are. Writers and researchers during many generations to come undoubtedly will analyze and consider those later questions and prophesies.

In the meantime, however, there's another timely and important task to address now, today. That's how to prepare for the tribulation period mentioned in Daniel and Revelation. We have been given clues as to when it will occur; at the midpoint of an established peace pact by seven nations. And the 'rider of the black horse' went forth to warn us of the many shortages of items, particularly items that cause hunger and famine. The Book of Revelation has warned us. It has revealed many things.

Chapter 11
The Tribulation

That time of tribulation is mentioned several times in the Bible. And, there are some general clues about the time and the events. The first mention in Revelation of a tribulation is in one of the seven letters John wrote to the Seven Churches in Asia, now Turkey. The mention of tribulation was in the letter to Thyatira; and it was regarding that woman; Jezebel. That was revealed in Chapter 2, beginning with Verse 20:

"Notwithstanding I have a few things against thee, because thou sufferest that woman, Jezebel, which calleth herself a prophetess, to teach and to seduce my servants to commit fornication, and to eat things sacrificed unto idols. 21, And I gave her space to repent of her fornication; and she repented not. 22, Behold, I will cast her into a bed, and them that commit adultery with her into great tribulation, except they repent of their deeds."

From reading earlier chapters in this book, you already know that the word 'Jezebel' is a metaphor for a religion; the Islamic religion. The different emphasis in these verses is that those who 'sufferest' Islam, meaning supporting and giving comfort to Islam (not necessarily 'suffering from' which might be the interpreted meaning,) will be considered as having committed adultery with her. That means they will suffer the 'great' tribulation. This reading suggests those who aren't captured by Islam's lies and deceptions, although they will suffer through a tribulation; it will not be a great tribulation. And, there will be many deceptions to lure believers away from the true Christ to this false one, this Jezebel, in the end times. Matthew 24:4-5 reveals one of those warnings:

"Tell us, when will these things be, and what will be the sign of your coming and of the close of the age?" And Jesus answered them, "See that no one leads you astray. For many will come in my name, saying, 'I am the Christ,' and they will lead many astray." Matthew continues the warning not to be deceived in 24: 22-28:

"And except those days should be shortened, there should no flesh be saved: but for the elect's sake those shall be shortened. Then if any man shall say unto you, Lo, here is Christ, or there; believe it not. For there shall arise false Christs, and false prophets, and shall shew great signs and wonders; insomuch that, if it were possible they shall deceive the very elect. Behold, I have told you before. Wherefore if they shall say unto you Behold, he is in the desert; go not forth: behold, he is in the secret chambers, believe it not. For as the lightning cometh out of the east, and shineth even unto the west; so shall also the coming of the Son of man be. For wheresoever the carcase is, there will the eagles (or buzzards) be gathered together."

The comment above, "they shall deceive the very elect" seemingly innocuous, is very important. It suggests that those false prophets and false Christs of Islam will be so influential politically that they will influence the very halls of those we choose to protect us. Could it mean some will be elected over us to become our leaders and those whose responsibility is to protect us; even from that very beast appointed over us? That's already happening in many countries that beast has targeted to attack; even already in the United States, the country most capable of world protection. In this case our leadership is strongly failing us that will lead us closer to that time of tribulation. Verses 19-31 of Matthew reveal even more; a sign of the end of that tribulation period, when Christ shows himself:

"Immediately after the tribulation of those days the sun will be darkened, and the moon will not give its light, and the stars will fall from heaven, and the powers of the heavens will be shaken. Then will appear in heaven the sign of the Son of Man, and then all the tribes of the earth will mourn, and they will see the Son of Man coming on the clouds of heaven with power and great glory. And he will send out his angels with a loud trumpet call, and they will gather his elect from the four winds, from one end of heaven to the other."

Okay, we know basically what the tribulation is; a time of harshness and death. The great tribulation will be mainly against the followers of that false religion, Islam; and unfortunately Islam's primary target of Israel. However, others will suffer to some degree, mainly from famine and thirst. But, when will it begin? According to Daniel 9:25-27, it will begin midway the duration of an agreement, a covenant with many. It begins:

"Know therefore and understand, that from the going forth of the commandment to restore and to build Jerusalem unto the Messiah the Prince shall be seven weeks, and threescore and two weeks: the street shall be built again, and the wall, even in troublous times. And after threescore and two weeks shall Messiah be cut off, but not for himself: and the people of the prince (note lower case p which represents one other than Christ; a deceiver) that shall come shall destroy the city and the sanctuary; and the end thereof shall be with a flood, and unto the end of the war desolations are determined.

And he shall confirm the covenant with many for one week (seven years): and in the midst of the week he shall cause the sacrifice and the oblation to cease, and for the overspreading of abominations he shall make it desolate, even until the consummation, and that determined shall be poured upon the desolate." (They will 'flee unto the hills.')

Could this pertain to the new nuclear arms agreement with Iran?

Daniel 9:27 says an agreement will be made for seven years (one week) among seven leaders (5+1+Iran) and at the 'midst' of that agreement it will be abandoned. Further information reveals Israel will be attacked which will create the 'Abomination of Desolation' and the great tribulation. The times of tribulation will create extreme famine and many other horrible events. According to further information, those horrors will last three and a half years; the last half of the agreement that was abandoned. How sudden and severe will it be for some? Matthew 24:17-21 gives that warning:

"When ye therefore shall see the abomination of desolation, spoken of by Daniel the prophet, stand in the holy place, (whoso readeth, let him understand:) Then let them which be in Judae'a flee into the mountains: Let him which is on the house top not come down to take any thing out of his house: Neither let him which is in the field return back to take his clothes. And woe unto them that are with child, and to them that suck in those days! But pray ye that your flight be not in the winter, neither on the sabbath day: For then there will be great tribulation, such as has not been from the beginning of the world until now, no, and never will be."

When that great war begins, or when serious preparations are nearly complete for that war (for example while Iran finishes preparation for that nuclear attack against Israel which the seven great nations have allowed; 'those who letteth will let') what will happen to earthly things? For certain, survival and life events will not be as they are today. Most certainly, the first impact will be the restricted oil and gas supply, and skyrocketing prices. Eventually, the average worker will not afford to buy enough gas to get to work, since many workers today must commute many miles to get to their job sites; or perhaps the job is even traveling in a vehicle. This, in itself, will create a great crisis.

All commerce will cease immediately in the Middle East, the Muslim countries, in accordance with Revelation 18:21 that states: "And a mighty angel took up a stone like a great millstone, and cast it into the sea, saying, Thus with violence shall that great city Babylon be thrown down..." This sea is not referring to a body of water; it's referring to a sea of humanity - people. Adding to the confusion will be the enmity still raging between the two Islamic divisions; the Sunni and the Shiite.

The Shiite, led by Iran, is still most determined to create a vicious war with Israel to force their Mahdi to appear from occultation to make the world pure - pure Muslim. This is the basis of the difference between the two divisions of Islam, and it explains why Iran is supporting the Islamic radicals and terrorists as fully as they are. In accordance with their Islamic beliefs, if they create enough horror and turmoil, the Mahdi will have no choice but to show himself and fulfill the Islamic promise - to make everyone in the world a Muslim. Therefore, the Iranians and their Shiite brethren will never accept any peace proposal that disallows them from 'ridding Israel from the face of the earth.' Those who believe otherwise have their heads stuck deep in the sand - or cement.

And, this is a very important point. The radical clerical leaders in those Muslim countries don't really care what happens to their followers; it's okay if they all kill themselves in acts of martyrdom. Their only goal is to establish their personal positions of power, and to bring the Mahdi out from occultation to make the whole world follow and worship that beast - Islam. Is it a power thing, or a religious thing? Adolph Hitler promoted himself as building a greater world for mankind. How many people did he kill and have killed in that grand design?

As a side note: The Sunni, as the Jewish religion, don't believe their Messiah has yet appeared. They are still waiting for him to appear the first time. To them, their Mahdi is not already here, waiting in occultation to appear and 'save the world.' It seems this is a concept they have copied from the Jewish and Christian religions.

Nevertheless, with their common hatred of Israel, all Muslims will likely join forces against Israel once the battle begins. How can the world allow this great battle to happen? This is explained in 2 Thessalonians. It begins in verse 3:

"Let no man deceive you by any means; for that day shall not come, except there come a falling away first, and that man of sin be revealed, the son of perdition; 4, Who opposeth and exalteth himself above all that is called God, or that is worshiped; so that he as God sitteth in the temple of God, shewing himself that he is God."

This is an explanation of the abomination of desolation. This will happen at the mid-point of an established seven-year treaty or pact, when the treaty will be flung aside by the beast. The agreement will be formed by 'seven kings.' (The seven years is interpreted from the word 'week.' The length of the agreement could be different.)

In current terms, this means there will be a falling away from God, and from the obligation of a Godly nation, or power, to stand with Israel in time of peril. In the past, our government has maintained a pledge, and has let the whole world know that an attack against Israel would be treated the same as an attack against the United States; which was founded on the basic principles of those acknowledged by Israel - the belief in and worship of God. This explains one concept of 'falling away.'

The 'blasphemer and deceiver' who now sits in the White House of our great nation has already expressed his disdain for Israel; and his pure love of Islam. Is he the one who creates the falling away? Certainly he's the one, in that high leadership position, with the greatest indications of being anti-Israel; of falling away. No one else on the world scene can be seen as having the authority and position to allow this to happen.

Verse 6 continues, "And now ye know what withholdeth that he might be revealed in his time. 7, For the mystery of iniquity doth already work: only he who now letteth will let, until he be taken out of the way. 8, And then shall that Wicked be revealed, whom the Lord shall consume with the spirit of his mouth and shall destroy with the brightness of his coming."

The key phrase here is, "only he who now letteth will let, until he be taken out of the way." As cited above, the United States has protected Israel, because of sharing the same basis for existence; the worship of God, and because of the common cultural principles guiding our daily lives. This quote says that the one who could let evil attack Israel will do just that; he will allow evil to attack that great nation. This leader who worships one other than the God of Gods will allow Israel to be attacked. That will start that great war known as the Battle of Armageddon. According to the other parts of Revelation, that will be Islam's greatest mistake; they will be totally consumed. But, in the meantime there will be much tribulation throughout the whole world.

Then the scripture says who will be consumed: 9, "Even him, whose coming is after the working of Satan with all power and signs and lying wonders". (That antichrist - that beast, also known as the blasphemer and deceiver. One lives among us at this time who blasphemes God, and spews many lies, falsehoods, and deceptions.) 10, "And with all deceivableness and unrighteousness in them that perish, because they received not the love of the truth, that they might be saved. 11, And for this cause God shall send them strong delusion, that they should believe a lie. 12, That they all might be damned who believed not the truth, but had pleasure in unrighteousness." (Those who followed and worshiped that beast, that antichrist; that ungodly religion.)

The people of that area, the Islamic nations, those who survive, will be void of any commerce; and will likely return to that life of the old days; wandering Bedouins. But, they will be wandering Bedouins who will understand; and will praise the real God; the First and the

169

Last; Alpha and Omega. The soul of the one who led them astray, that antichrist Mohammad, and the soul of the false prophet will join Satan in the 'lake of fire and brimstone, and shall be tormented day and night for ever and ever.' Chapter 20, Verse 10. After a thousand years, Satan will rise again to challenge the power of God; and this will be Satan's last great battle. He will then be cast into the burning pit where he will remain forever and forever.

Their millstone will have been destroyed. Those Muslims will have destroyed their possible great future by 'going forward with a great sword to take peace from the earth,' according to Chapter 6, Verse 4. That blasphemer and deceiver will have led them through the gates of Hell. Perhaps he's not the one who led them through the gates of Hell, but he certainly will pave the way for them to find Hell by themselves.

Understanding how devastating the results of that great battle will be, everyone on earth will be effected. Life as we know it will change; and outside that war zone it will be mostly from the loss of normal commerce and transportation. Shortages of food in many places will cause much famine; lack of common supplies and tools will cripple industry, and insecurity on major highways will curtail transportation access that we consider normal today. Let's consider a few possible examples; and according to information in Revelation, the situation could be even much worse than in these examples:

First, let's consider food. Much of our stable vegetable, fruit, and nut supply traditionally came from California. Today, much of our food comes from Central and South America. Whether it comes from California or South America it requires an integrated transportation system to disperse it all over the United States. Consider what would happen if:

1. Oil from the Middle East suddenly ceased.

2. Integrated parts for manufacture or repair of food production, farm, equipment were not available because manufacturers lacked energy to produce those parts.

3. The price of available oil doubled or tripled due to demand and availability, making transportation of food unprofitable.

4. Petroleum products and other chemicals and fertilizers were not available, or could not be delivered, to feed and nourish local food growth.

5. Cattle feed could not be distributed due to lack of dependable transportation, or it couldn't be produced and cultivated.

6. Workdays were limited to daylight hours due to lack of fuel to produce enough electricity; that available energy source would have to be allocated to higher priorities.

7. Food required to be refrigerated for transportation or storage could not be preserved in that environment.

8. Enough energy was not produced, or was not timely effective to allow safe storage in home refrigerators or freezers.

9. Mechanical farm equipment, including harvesters and pickers, was not available to process food from the ground, stalk, or trees.

10. Grain elevators and other mechanized storage facilities did not have energy to load, protect, and dispense those stored products.

That absence of oil from the Middle East (or the distribution and delivery thereof) would have many other devastating effects world-wide that can't be anticipated at this time. The reference below mentions ships and the sea, but the connotation of 'sea' in Revelation also refers to 'sea' of people and humanity; therefore consider major highways as part of that sea.

Revelation specifically mentions shipping and ship masters in Chapter 18. Verse 17 begins that specific identification: "For in one hour so great riches is come to nought, And every shipmaster, and all the company in ships, and sailors, and as many as trade by the sea, stood afar off, 18, And cried when they saw the smoke of her burning,…19…wherein were made rich all that had ships in the sea by reason of her costliness! For in one hour is she made desolate."

Not only would a lack of or shortage of oil affect shipping; the absence of the ability to process and manufacture items when delivered would curtail much shipping. Many places of the whole world would become desolate.

Famine would become a major problem throughout the whole world. Many parts of Africa that traditionally suffer famine would have the 'death of humanity and beasts' strewn about for hundreds of square miles, or more.

Survival would once again become the nature of humanity. Prosperity and comfort would be abandoned and forgotten. Perhaps those in the 'sea' identified as 'preppers' are the ones most prepared according to the warnings; and there are two clear and distinct warnings in Revelation.

First is the warning to the Church at Sardis (all churches):

"Be watchful, and strengthen the things which remain, that are ready to die; for I have not found thy works perfect before God. Remember therefore how thou hast received and heard, and hold fast, and repent. If therefore thou shalt not watch, I will come on thee as a thief, and thou shalt not know what hour I will come upon thee."

Second is that final warning in Revelation Chapter 16, Verse 15:

"Behold, I come as a thief. Blessed is he that watcheth, and keepeth his garments, lest he walk naked, and they see his shame."

At this point, one must ask why Barack Obama and his administration criticize preppers and others who read and trust the words of the Bible as 'dangerous right-wing nuts.' Why does he, and others who follow him, worship him, and promote his principles of Islam and anarchy despise and reject those led by the principles long ago written in the Bible - from experiences through much shed blood? Why are they so fearful of, and so viciously attack that Word of God?

And the question must be asked: Why does Barack Obama so adamantly refuse to allow development of our own abundant supply of oil and other natural resources to alleviate these hardships when they begin? What is his purpose for refusing American security? Does he know something; and is supporting it? Even with his dogmatic war against self-sufficient energy through more open oil drilling areas, natural gas, and coal production, America has achieved almost self-sufficient status. And, the United States could probably achieve that full self-sufficiency within a short time, not having to function under his dogmatic restrictions.

Even if the United States became self-sufficient in energy production, that still would not solve the world-wide crisis that would occur. Any crisis in the rest of the production and manufacturing world would affect the United States as well as other countries that depend on oil for their existence. Canada, China, India, Japan, and Europe would be totally defenseless, and without power resources even to exist within a reasonable condition of normal humanity. So, what pressures would that create for the oil produced in the United States. Would the United States share, or would the United States struggle to exist within itself? Could the United States prosper without other parts of the world prospering?

A similar event was reported in Ezekiel concerning the Philistines,

Moab, Edom and Tyrus. Chapter 25:15, begins the pertinent information:

"Thus saith the Lord God; Because the Philistines have dealt by revenge, and have taken vengeance with a despiteful heart, to destroy it (Israel) for the old hatred. 16, Therefore, thus saith the Lord God; Behold, I will stretch out mine hand upon the Philistines, and I will cut off the Cherethims, and destroy the remnant of the sea coast." The next verses explain the devastation to follow:

Verse 17: "And I will execute great vengeance upon them with furious rebukes; and they shall know that I am the Lord, when I shall lay my vengeance upon them." The following verses describe many of the devastating events from King Nebuchadnezzar of Babylon upon them:

"He shall slay with the sword thy daughters in the field. And, he shall set engines of war against thy walls. He shall slay thy people by the sword. And they shall make a spoil of their riches, and make a prey of thy merchandise. And I will cause the noise of thy songs to cease; and the sound of harps shall be no more."

Verse 16, "Then all the princes of the sea shall come down from their thrones, and lay away their robes, and put off their broidered garments; they shall clothe themselves with trembling; they shall sit upon the ground, and shall tremble at every moment, and be astonished at thee."

Chapter 27 continues to explain the devastation of that nation. It mentions things such as: a merchant of the people for many isles, trees from Senir and cedars from Lebanon to make ships and masts, oaks from Bashan to make oars, benches of ivory from Chittim, fine linen from Egypt to make sails, and those of blue and purple for clothing.

This list of merchandise that will no longer be available continues in more verses: riches of silver, iron, tin, and lead from Tarshish; men and vessels of brass from Javan, Tubal, and Meshech; horsemen, horses, and mules from Togarmah; and emeralds, purple, and broidered work, and fine linen, and coral, and agate from Syria. The list of items and their sources continues through verse 36. Now, one might ask, 'why is this comparable information important?' (Here the color purple is listed, but it's associated with broidered work which means fabric. Purple dye was an important item at that time. But, this list does not mention the colors red or scarlet.)

It's important for two reasons. First, it reinforces the idea that a war can wreak havoc in areas other than the location of the actual combat. Secondly, it's an example that God will defend and protect Israel against those who show no respect for His existence or for the existence of Israel. Also, isn't it quite interesting that the name Babylon was used in both these situations? One identifies the kingdom of Nebuchadnezzar; one identifies the kingdom, that religion of Islam.

And, we must not forget that word mentioned twice in Revelation; it's likely the same condition that happened during this comparable event detailed in Ezekial. That word is 'famine.' Although the word famine was not mentioned in John's letters to the seven churches, one admonition was given to all seven churches - and to all churches. That admonition is; 'He that hath an ear, pay attention and don't get embarrassed because you are found unprepared and naked.'

Hunger and famine are mentioned three times in Revelation. First is from the description of the rider of the pale horse in 6:8: "...to kill with sword, and with hunger, and with death, and with the beasts of the earth." 'Beasts of the earth' possibly involves pestilence; it might also include those long-ago beasts that now rise from the earth in the form of oil. That' also a likely source of darkness covering the sun and the moon as oil wells and distribution facilities are destroyed and

175

burned throughout the Middle East.

Next is from 18:8, which reads: "Therefore shall her plagues come in one day, death, and mourning, and famine..."

The reference in Chapter 13 is more subtle. It's related to the 'mark of the beast' in verse 17, which is written: "And that no man might buy or sell, save he that had the mark, or the name of the beast, or the number of his name." Further reading clearly warns that if anyone accepts the mark of the beast, becomes a Muslim, he will be excluded from the 'book of life' and will not be worthy to join Christ in Heaven. This refers back to Chapter 6:17 where souls waiting to be redeemed are asking 'how much longer?" This is when the fifth seal was opened.

Verse 11 answers the question regarding 'how much longer' and the mark of the beast, "...that they should rest yet for a little season, until their fellowservants also and their brethren, that should be killed as they were, should be fulfilled." This will happen to many of those who refuse to accept the mark of the beast that will allow them to buy food and other necessities of life. At that time, a great choice one must make; to preserve human life on earth or to allow life eternal with Christ.

Many signs and signals suggest that time of tribulation and great tribulation might be near; fast approaching. Christ reminds of this in the last chapter of Revelation; Chapter 22:

Verse 6: "And he said unto me, These sayings are faithful and true: and the Lord God of the holy prophets sent his angel to shew unto his servants the things which must shortly be done."

Verse 7: "Behold, I come quickly: blessed is he that keepeth the sayings of the prophecy of this book."

Verse 12: "And, behold, I come quickly; and my reward is with me, to give every man according as his work shall be."

Finally, in the last verses of Revelation His Word reminds us again to hold fast. He also reminds us to beware of those blasphemers and deceivers who lie to persuade us otherwise; those who say they are Jews, but are not; including that prophetess Jezebel.

Verse 14: "Blessed are they that do his commandments, that they may have right to the tree of life, and may enter in through the gates into the city."

Verse 15: "For without are dogs, and sorcerers, and whoremongers, and murderers, and idolaters, and whosoever loveth and maketh a lie."

Be prepared. Food to prevent famine; and pure water to prevent thirst will be most critical and important during this time of tribulation. Otherwise, why would this prophetic Book of Revelation speak of these things?

Chapter 12
The Silent Jihad

M any concepts and ideas presented by Islam, and supported at this time by Barack Obama, don't fit into the natural discussion of the Book of Revelation. However, they are very important in understanding Islam's concepts of today. Before we begin these related considerations, one must keep in mind a very important premise:

According to God's Word in the Book of Revelation: there are no peaceful Muslims. Revelation clearly explains that Islam itself is based on the worship of Satan, and regardless of the actions of any individual Muslim, peaceful or radical, that religion still worships and promotes Satan.

Satan is the entity constantly trying to eliminate God from the lives of true believers. Satan; through the belief, words, and actions of his followers - all Muslims, intends to destroy and replace God. Satan spoke that intention when he said 'the end of these things' - God's things, "which are therein, that there should be time no longer." (Revelation 10:6.) Chapter 12 makes that crystal clear, specifically after Satan failed, through King Herod, to kill baby Jesus and the Christian religion that followed. Verse 17 is very clear and specific; crystal clear:

"And the dragon was wroth with the woman (Christianity) and went to make war with the remnant of her seed, which keep the commandments of God, and have the testimony of Jesus Christ."

In other words, Satan will never quit his activity to destroy God, Christ and Christianity. At the moment Satan is using the Islamic religion to do his bidding; the goal he failed at the beginning of Christ. As Chapter 17 relates: Islam is the mother of harlot radicals, and harlot radicals are Mother Islam's daughter. Therefore; they are one and the same. Those radicals, the 'whore' must protect, defend, and promote their mother religion. They exist together. The radicals will exist as long as the mother religion, who worships Satan, exists. Perhaps many are peaceful as individuals; but their basic foundation is to support Satan in his long quest to replace God. The peaceful ones are as guilty as the most radical ones.

And, two verses reveal they will kill one another. This has been explained earlier in this book. Now, understanding that Islam is Islam, whether mother or harlot radical, we will continue with more important information. First we will review the basic tenets of Islam; that expressed in their Sharia Law. Sharia Law over the whole world is their goal; other than making the whole world Muslim - without one having a choice. Now, would a god of peace really support these elements of Sharia Law?

This is part of Islam's Sharia Law:

1. Theft is punishable by cutting off the right hand. But, there is no mention of who makes that determination, or how that determination is made. According to past examples, that determination and execution is made by the one in power. In this case, how is justice insured?

2. Criticizing or denying any part of the Quran is punishable by death. So, where are the peaceful Muslims to insure justice? Where is the freedom of speech that free and godly people are allowed to enjoy?

3. Criticizing or denying Muhammad is a prophet is punishable by death. Again, where is free speech and justice under the law?

4. Criticizing or denying Allah, (their Allah that began as the pagan moon god) is punishable by death. Within this, where is there peace and freedom to discuss anything without being put in harm's way?

5. A Muslim who becomes a non-Muslim is punishable by death. Does this indicate or suggest anything about being peaceful; or believing that Muslims and Christians worship the same god. If we worship the same god (God) then why aren't we allowed to worship Him by another name?

6. A non-Muslim who leads a Muslim away from Islam is punishable by death. Does this not suggest an unloving god who demands he be worshiped and not a God who offers, not demands, salvation and true paradise? Could this in any way be considered peaceful?

7. A non-Muslim man who marries a Muslim woman is punishable by death. Would a real god who cared about love, family, and worship really demand this?

8. A man can marry a young girl at any age and consummate the marriage when she is only 9 years old. Is there any abomination greater than this? This is only one of the many abominations attached to that false religion in Revelation. Not only is this an abomination - any person with human and godly feeling would consider it reprehensible. But Islam?

9. Muhammad's words in Book 41, Kitab Al-Adab, Hadith 5251 says a girl's clitoris should be cut. Why do Muslims focus so heavily on sex to illusion young men to kill themselves? Even their martyrs are promised 72 virgins when they accomplish horrible acts against non-Muslims. How, in any way whatsoever, can this be involved with peace? Sex and power; is that their guiding preamble?

10. Muslim women can have 1 husband, but a man can have up to 4 wives. Muhammad can have even more. Again, is this not the male part of Islam so focused on sex that he justifies a harem for himself?

11. A man can divorce his wife anytime and without a reason, but a woman has to have her husband's consent to divorce. This one is totally beyond any kind of understanding or comprehension; other than a Muslim man may keep his imprisoned harem as long as he desires. Interesting that a Muslim woman would consider this as peaceful. Would it not otherwise be considered bondage?

12. A man may beat his wife for insubordination. Maybe this beating in to persuade her to become a Muslim of 'peace.'

13. Four male witnesses must testify to prove rape against a woman. Just curious; has a Muslim man ever been convicted of rape against a Muslim woman? Hardly.

14. A woman who has been raped cannot testify in court against those who raped her. Does this not suggest that Muslim men have an open range harem; where they can command sex from any woman they meet, and the woman cannot defend herself or get justice? Again; that dizzying focus on sex, sex, sex.

15. A woman's testimony in court, allowed only in property cases, carries only half the value or importance of a man's. This is certainly justice guaranteed.

16. A woman heir inherits only half of what a man heir inherits. Their Allah is not only so peaceful; he is also so very fair and equitable.

17. A woman cannot drive a car, as it leads to fitnah (upheaval). Or she might use the car to make her well-deserved escape from bondage and abomination. But, even if they escape; where can they go for

refuge?

18: A woman cannot speak alone to a man who is not her husband or relative. The Muslim man must keep his harem tightly controlled in a corralled environment.

19. Meat to be eaten must come from animals that have been sacrificed to Allah. It must be Halal food. Halal foods are those things sacrificed to the moon god idol that still sits in Mecca. That idol is represented by pieces of a black meteorite rock located in the 'black cube.' God warns against eating food sacrificed to idols. Certainly, a moon god and a black rock would not be considered idols, according to this belief.

20. Muslims are allowed and even encouraged to engage in Taqiyya and lie to non-Muslims to advance, justify, and promote Islam. Lying, falsehoods, and deceptions are encouraged if the aim is to protect Islam and to spread its influence. So what's new. Their whole religion is based on and begins with Taqiyya: that their religion is a religion of 'peace.'

Islam began as worship to a pagan god

John's letters were not intended only for those Christians in the churches in Asia at that time. All seven letters to those seven churches are as important today as they were at the time they were written; even more important because they have more meaning and focus today. Summarized, they say: "Those who have an ear, pay attention and don't be deceived away from your faith." Much of the following information from John regarded the Islamic religion. Where did that religion start?

Roddy Newman from Islam-Watch.org, published this article on 11 October, 2011, titled: Allah Was Originally a Pre-Muslim Arabian

"Moon God."

"When Islamists engage in terrorism, or use political power to introduce Sharia law, they do so because they have faith in Allah, allegedly the Omnipotent God. So, it is important to explain to them that Allah was originally a pre-Muslim Arabian "Moon god". Modern Islamists, of course, have no idea that they worship a "Moon god"; instead they see Allah as a God, Who is the Creator of the universe. But their delusion does not alter the fact that Allah was originally a lunar deity as I will now explain.

To this day, Allah's "Moon god" origins are visible on the tops of countless mosques, for example on the tops of the twin towers of the Great Mosque in Mecca, where you can see the "crescent Moon" symbol, which represented the "Moon god" in the Ancient Middle East. The crescent Moon symbol is also on the top of the Maqam Ibrahim structure beside Mecca's Kaba shrine, which is the holiest place in the world for Muslims. Finally, the same symbol is on the flags of some mostly-Muslim nations (Algeria, Azerbaijan, Malaysia, the Maldives, Mauritania, Pakistan, Turkey, and Uzbekistan), on the flag which Libya's National Transitional Council have adopted, and on the sides of the ambulances which the Muslim equivalent of the Red Cross (the Red Crescent) operate, though those flags, and the Red Crescent emblem, were thought up long after Muslims began putting symbols of Allah the Moon god on the tops of their early mosques, and are thus, unlike those mosques, not proof of Allah's Moon god origins.

Like the pre-Christian Roman Empire, which was run by people, who worshiped outer space deities like Jupiter and Mars, pre-Muslim Middle Eastern peoples worshiped heavenly bodies like the Moon, because they were in awe of the big objects they saw in outer space, and did not know what they were, as they did not have modern astronomical knowledge, which led them to decide that the big objects in outer space were deities who should be worshiped.

In the Ancient Middle East, worship of the Moon god under such names as Suen and Sin (and of course Allah) was common, so common in fact that the writers of "The Old Testament" felt the need to condemn lunar deity worship in several places (Deuteronomy 4:19, and 17:3, II Kings 21:3 and 5, and 23:5, Jeremiah 8:2, and 19:13, and Zephaniah 1:5). The scorching summer heat of that part of the world, possibly made many locals decide that the Sun, which was worshiped as a god or goddess in other places, was not their big friend in outer space, unlike the Moon god who appeared during the night, when the heat of the day abated.

The worship of the "Moon god" continued into the Christian era in pre-Muslim Arabia, where people in Mecca worshiped their lunar deity, Allah, at the Kaba shrine. Many gods and goddesses were worshiped in pre-Islamic Mecca, but Allah, who was seen as the father of other gods and goddesses, was the Supreme Deity.

The Kaba shrine contains a famous black meteorite, which landed at the site of what became Mecca. Pre-Muslim Arabians revered the space rock, as they did not know what meteorites were, which led them to believe that their Supreme Deity had sent them the rock. So, they built the Kaba shrine to Allah at the meteorite's impact site. Mecca then developed around the Moon god's shrine, because the desert Bedouins made pilgrimages to the place, where they thought Allah had sent them a space rock.

The fact that Muslims regard what was primarily a shrine to a pre-Muslim lunar deity as their holiest place is, of course, further proof that Allah was originally a "Moon god". Why did Mohammed not build a new shrine for the God of his new religion instead of simply taking over one, which was already devoted to Allah the "Moon god"?

The fact that, to this day, when Muslims make their pilgrimage to Mecca, they kiss or touch the black meteorite in the Kaba, which is yet more proof that Allah was originally a lunar deity. Why did Mohammed not create a new "holy relic" for Muslims to kiss or touch, instead of telling them to kiss or touch Allah the Moon god's "holy relic"?

Although the word "Allah" simply means "God", the fact that Muhammad did not invent a new name for his new Muslim god when he invented Islam is, of course, even more proof that Allah was originally a lunar deity. There is no debate about the fact that the Moon god worshiping Meccans referred to their supreme deity as Allah before Mohammed, which is why a man called Abd-Allah – meaning "servant of Allah", or "slave of Allah" – lived in Mecca before Muhammad and that man was very likely Muhammad's father.

He was presumably called Abd-Allah, because his Banu Hashim clansmen of the Quraysh tribe were pious devotees of their Moon god, as they were in charge of looking after the Kaba shrine.

Abd-Allah was not given a new Muslim name after Muhammad invented Islam, because Abd-Allah died 6 months before Muhammad was born. Moreover, even Muhammad had given one of his sons the name Abd-Allah well before he began inventing Islam at the age of 40 by writing the "Koran." End of article.

Stages of the Jihad

While one head of the evil serpent violently attacks us, and threatens more attacks against us, the other head slips in the back door to institutionalize its ugly evil. The Muslim Brotherhood had wide, deep and long tentacles that reach into every nook and cranny to destroy our freedom, our democracy, and our future well-being. These are those peaceful Muslims.

According to Civilus Defendus 'with a hat tip to Kali Politus' at

Wordpress.com, there's a standard process of Islamic encroachment to occupy and take over a non-Islamic nation. The article is titled, '4 Stages of Islamic Conquest.' And, there's another Muslim Brotherhood plan discovered in 1991, titled, 'An Explanatory Memorandum: On the General Strategic Goal for the Group In North America.' That plan will be reviewed after this article by Wordpress.

Those four stages reported by Wordpress.com and the tactics to enforce or implement those stages are explained:

"The first stage is infiltration:

In this stage Muslims begin moving into non-Muslim countries. Their numbers gradually increase at first, and with little or no visible conflicts. Those conflicts that exist are, at first, very subtle. They begin to fit in and ask the host country to be more understanding since they are peaceful, and only victims or where they came from. They continue to claim they are peaceful, although more conflicts between cultures continue to rise. They appeal for more tolerance.

As the size and numbers of more Muslim families increase, they begin to increase in their population and influence; more mosques are built to support those larger populations. Then those mosques become the birthplaces to spread more Islam and to begin exclaiming the stronger Islamic ideologies, and more hatred for the host countries and the historical culture of those host countries.

Once partially established as a part of the community they claim they are being persecuted by 'Islamophobia' and increase their insistence that anyone using Islamophobia against them should be charged with a hate crime. Their further reaction is to threaten legal action against individuals and groups for discrimination and hate crimes. Finally, they propose more interfaith discussions for a better understanding between religions. This is the subterfuge toward more Islamic

187

indoctrination to continue their settlement." The Wordpress article continues:

"How many nations are suffering from Islamic infiltration? One? A handful? Nearly every nation? The Islamic leadership of the Muslim Brotherhood and others wish to dissolve each nation's sovereignty and replace it with the global imposition of Islamic sharia law. Sharia law, based on the koran, sira and hadith, condemns liberty and forbids equality and is inconsistent with the laws of all Western nations. As the author and historian Serge Trifkovic states:

'The refusal of the Western elite class to protect their nations from jihadist infiltration is the biggest betrayal in history.'"

The second stage is consolidation of power:

This is the phase, the stage where Muslim 'settlers' begin to make their presence more obvious; where they begin to demand more rights, more Islamic freedom, and more acceptance from the local society - although they try to separate themselves through that acceptance. This is as absurd as a Muslim female asking to be free in that Muslim society in which she exists. To stress this point further this is a good time to ask that question:

(If a Muslim female is subjected by Islamic doctrine to be assaulted, maimed, abused, disregarded as a human, and actually killed, in the name of Islam - how can Islam proclaim itself to be 'The religion of Peace?" No other religion, no other country, no other real human being in this world would consider those actions as acts of 'peace.' By its own writings and proclamations, Islamists destroy the foundational basis of their existence. How could terrorizing one person, a female, or a whole nation be considered an act of 'peace?')

That Wordpress article adds this list of accelerated activities by the new Muslim communities:

"Muslim immigrants and host country converts continue demands for accommodation in employment, education, social services, financing and courts."

Even further: Proselytizing increases; Establishment and Recruitment of Jihadi cells begin; There are increased efforts to convert alienated segments of the population to Islam; Muslim leaders revise history to create more Islam into our backgrounds, and they begin to destroy the real evidence that exposes what true Islam really is.

Other subversive and 'settlement' activities include: Increasing negative propaganda against Western history; sweeping up other anti-American groups to give more strength to their operations and tactics against American status-quo. They also begin to infiltrate school systems and other teaching and influencing areas to bring children into their Islamic ideology for continued expansion of their mission. Their settlement strategies and tactics never let up; they continue onward to fulfill that grand design of world Islamism.

They increase their charge to silence their non-Muslims detractors opponents by intimidation and by other charges, such as blasphemy against Islam. They increase their emphasis and growing influence to push for more hate laws against those who oppose their plan and expose their real purpose; which is to make the land they occupy into a purely Muslim nation. According to their own writings and ideologies, they cannot be real Muslims if they stray from this final goal. Activities in this second stage also include the following:

* Efforts to introduce blasphemy and hate laws in order to silence critics.

* Continued focus on enlarging Muslim population by increasing Muslim births and immigration.

* Use of charities to recruit supporters and fund jihad.

* Covert efforts to bring about the destruction of host society from within.

* Development of Muslim political base in non-Muslim host society.

* Islamic Financial networks fund political growth, acquisition of land.

* Highly visible assassination of critics aimed to intimidate opposition.

* Tolerance of non-Muslims diminishes.

* Greater demands to adopt strict Islamic conduct.

* Clandestine amassing of weapons and explosives in hidden locations.

* Overt disregard/rejection of non-Muslim society's legal system, culture.

* Efforts to undermine and destroy power base of non-Muslim religions including and especially Jews and Christians.

Is there a pattern here? Theo van Gogh is murdered in the Netherlands for 'insulting' Islam; the Organization of the Islamic Conference demands 'anti-blasphemy' laws through the United Nations; France is set afire regularly by 'youths' (read Muslims); the rise of (dis-) honor killings...holocaust denial...anti-Semitism...deception re the tenets of Islam; hatred toward Christians and Jews and Hindus and Buddhists. The pattern for all to see is the rise of Islamic intolerance and the covert/cultural jihad to remake host societies into sharia-compliant worlds – to remove host sovereignty and replace it with Islamic sharia law. Sharia law that condemns earthly liberty and individual freedom, that forbids equality among faiths and between the sexes, that rejects the concept of nations outside the global house of Islam, that of dar al-Islam. That Wordpress article continues with an explanation of stage three of the Islamization process.

The third stage is open war with leadership and culture:

* Open violence to impose Sharia law and associated cultural restrictions; rejection of host government, subjugation of other religions and customs.

* Intentional efforts to undermine the host government & culture.

* Acts of barbarity to intimidate citizens and foster fear and submission.

* Open and covert efforts to cause economic collapse of the society.

* All opposition is challenged and either eradicated or silenced.

* Mass execution of non-Muslims.

* Widespread ethnic cleansing by Islamic militias.

* Rejection and defiance of host society secular laws or culture.

* Murder of "moderate" Muslim intellectuals who don't support Islamization.

* Destruction of churches, synagogues and other non-Muslim institutions.

* Women are restricted further in accordance with Sharia law.

* Large-scale destruction of population, with assassinations and bombings.

* Toppling of government and usurpation of political power.

* Imposition of Sharia law.

The website www.thereligionofpeace.com keeps track of the number of violent jihad attacks as best it can. The site lists more than 14,000 attacks since September 2001. It is worth a visit. What is occurring, however, that is likely inestimable are events where muslims are bullied by other muslims for not being "muslim enough," where non-Muslims are intimidated into doing or not doing what they desire, where remnant populations are in a death spiral simply for being non-muslim in a predominantly muslim area. Christians, Jews, Hindus, Buddhists Animists and Atheists meet with death, property destruction or confiscation, forced conversion, rape, excessive taxation (the jizya), enslavement, riotous mobs and various other forms of islam (in-) justice at the hands of muslims in Sudan, Philippines, Kenya, Malaysia, India, etc. And let us not forget 'death to Apostates' the world over.

Stage 4: Totalitarian Islamic Theocracy:

Islam becomes the only religious-political-judicial-cultural ideology:

* Sharia becomes the law of the land.

* All non-Islamic human rights are cancelled.

* Enslavement and genocide of non-Muslim population.

Once Upon A Revelation: About Islam *Will Clark*

* Freedom of speech and the press eradicated.

* All religions other than Islam are forbidden and destroyed.

* Destruction of all evidence of non-Muslim culture, populations and symbols in country (Buddhas, houses of worship, art, etc).

The House of Islam ("peace"), dar al-Islam, includes those nations that have submitted to Islamic rule, to the soul crushing, liberty-condemning, discriminatory law of Sharia. The rest of the world is in the House of War, dar al-harb, because it does not submit to Sharia, and exists in a state of rebellion or war with the will of 'Allah.' No non-Muslim state or its citizens are "innocent," and remain viable targets of war for not believing in 'Allah.'

The Christian, Jewish, Coptic, Hindu and Zoroastrian peoples of the world have suffered under subjugation for centuries. The Dhimmi-esque are forbidden to construct houses of worship or repair existing ones, economically crippled by the heavy jizya (tax), socially humiliated, legally discriminated against, criminally targeted and generally kept in a permanent state of weakness, fear and vulnerability by Islamic governments.

It should be noted that forced conversions (Egypt) and slavery (Sudan) are still reported. Homosexuals have been hung in the public square in Iran. Young girls are married to old men. Apostates are threatened with death. "Honor" killings are routine. Women are legally second-class citizens, though Muslim males insist they are "treated better" than in the West. These more obvious manifestations may distract from some less obvious ones such as the lack of intellectual inquiry in science, narrow scope of writing, all but non-existent art and music, sexual use and abuse of youth and women, and the disregard for personal fulfillment, joy and wonder. Look into the eyes of a recently married 12 year old girl to see the consequence of the moral deprivation spawned by Islam." End of article by

Wordpress.com.

This information above explains the stages and steps as Muslims encroach and replace the foundations and cultures of a sovereign nation. But, how do they achieve these steps; how do they position themselves to accomplish those tactics? Their process is not secret. Muslim leaders have already boldly proclaimed how they will do it. Their plan is clearly laid out in the document identified as the Explanatory Memorandum. That memorandum describes the process of 'Settlement.' It's also commonly known as the 'Silent Jihad' or the 'Third Jihad.'

This direct and bloody Islamic jihad against America and all Western civilizations, that anyone who doesn't comply with radical Islamic ideology will be killed, is not the only Islamic war to control the United States and the rest of the world. There is also a more insidious plan to accomplish that ideological goal silently from within. Their plan is already well advanced in the United States. Many citizens know about it, but nothing is done to stop it. Barack Obama and his supporters seem to be facilitating this Islamic goal. This article from Discoverthenetworks.org gives an overview.

"In July 2007, seven key leaders of an Islamic charity known as the Holy Land Foundation for Relief and Development (HLF) went on trial for charges that they had: (a) provided "material support and resources" to a foreign terrorist organization (namely Hamas); (b) engaged in money laundering; and (c) breached the International Emergency Economic Powers Act, which prohibits transactions that threaten American national security. Along with the seven named defendants, the U.S. government released a list of approximately 300 "unindicted co-conspirators" and "joint venturers." During the course of the HLF trial, many incriminating documents were entered into evidence. Perhaps the most significant of these was "An Explanatory Memorandum on the General Strategic Goal for the Group in North America," by the Muslim Brotherhood operative Mohamed Akram.

Federal investigators found Akram's memo in the home of Ismael Elbarasse, a founder of the Dar Al-Hijrah mosque in Falls Church, Virginia, during a 2004 search. Elbarasse was a member of the Palestine Committee, which the Muslim Brotherhood had created to support Hamas in the United States.

Written sometime in 1987 but not formally published until May 22, 1991, Akram's 18-page document listed the Brotherhood's 29 likeminded "organizations of our friends" that shared the common goal of dismantling American institutions and turning the U.S. into a Muslim nation. These "friends" were identified by Akram and the Brotherhood as groups that could help convince Muslims "that their work in America is a kind of grand Jihad in eliminating and destroying the Western civilization from within and 'sabotaging' its miserable house by their hands ... so that ... God's religion [Islam] is made victorious over all other religions."

Akram was well aware that in the U.S., it would be extremely difficult to promote Islam by means of terror attacks. Thus the "grand jihad" that he and his Brotherhood comrades envisioned was not a violent one involving bombings and shootings, but rather a stealth (or "soft") jihad aiming to impose Islamic law (Sharia) over every region of the earth by incremental, non-confrontational means, such as working to "expand the observant Muslim base"; to "unif[y] and direc[t] Muslims' efforts"; and to "present Islam as a civilization alternative." At its heart, Akram's document details a plan to conquer and Islamize the United States – not as an ultimate objective, but merely as a stepping stone toward the larger goal of one day creating "the global Islamic state."

In line with this objective, Akram and the Brotherhood resolved to "settle" Islam and the Islamic movement within the United States, so that the Muslim religion could be "enabled within the souls, minds and the lives of the people of the country." Akram explained that this could be accomplished "through the establishment of firmly-rooted organizations on whose bases civilization, structure and testimony are built." He urged Muslim leaders to make "a shift from the collision mentality to the absorption mentality," meaning that they should abandon any tactics involving defiance or confrontation, and seek instead to implant into the larger society a host of seemingly benign Islamic groups with ostensibly unobjectionable motives; once those groups had gained a measure of public acceptance, they would be in a position to more effectively promote societal transformation by the old Communist technique of "boring from within."

"The heart and the core" of this strategy, said Akram, was contingent upon these groups' ability to develop "a mastery of the art of 'coalitions.' That is, by working synergistically they could complement, augment, and amplify one another's efforts. Added Akram: "The big challenge that is ahead of us is how to turn these seeds or 'scattered' elements into comprehensive, stable, 'settled' organizations that are connected with our Movement and which fly in our orbit and take orders from our guidance." The ultimate objective was not only an enlarged Muslim presence, but also implementation of the Brotherhood objectives of transforming pluralistic societies, particularly America, into Islamic states, and sweeping away Western notions of legal equality, freedom of conscience, freedom of religion, and freedom of speech.

Akram and the Brotherhood understood that in order to succeed in this endeavor, they needed to appeal to different strata of the American population in different ways; that whereas some people could be influenced by messages delivered from a religious perspective, others would be more responsive to messages delivered by educators, or bankers, or political figures, or journalists, etc. Thus, Akram's blueprint for the advancement of the Islamic movement stressed the need to form a coalition of groups coming from the worlds of education; religious proselytization; political activism; audio and video production; print media; banking and finance; the physical sciences; the social sciences; professional and business networking; cultural affairs; the publishing and distribution of books; children and teenagers; women's rights; vocational concerns; and jurisprudence.

By promoting the Islamic movement on such a wide variety of fronts, the Brotherhood and its allies could multiply exponentially their influence. Toward that end, the Akram/Brotherhood "Explanatory Memorandum" named the following 29 groups as the organizations they believed could collaborate effectively to destroy America from within – "if they all march according to one plan." This is that plan:

"In the name of God, the Beneficent, the Merciful Thanks be to God, Lord of the Two Worlds, Prayers and peace be upon the master of the Messengers:

An Explanatory Memorandum
On the General Strategic Goal for the Group In North America
5/22/1991

Contents:

1- An introduction in explanation
2- The Concept of Settlement
3- The Process of Settlement
4- Comprehensive Settlement Organizations

What might have encouraged me to submit the memorandum in this time in particular is my feeling of a "glimpse of hope" and the beginning of good tidings which bring the good news that we have embarked on a new stage of Islamic activism stages in this continent. The papers which are between your hands are not abundant extravagance, imaginations or hallucinations which passed in the mind of one of your brothers, but they are rather hopes, ambitions and challenges that I hope that you share some or most of which with me. I do not claim their infallibility or absolute correctness, but they are an attempt which requires study, outlook, detailing and rooting from you.

My request to my brothers is to read the memorandum and to write what they wanted of comments and corrections, keeping in mind that what is between your hands is not strange or a new submission without a root, but rather an attempt to interpret and explain some of what came in the long-term plan which we approved and adopted in our council and our conference in the year (1987).

Subject: A project for an explanatory memorandum for the General Strategic goal for the Group in North America mentioned in the long-term plan

One: The Memorandum is derived from:

1- The general strategic goal of the Group in America which was approved by the Shura Council and the Organizational Conference for the year [1987] is "Enablement of Islam in North America, meaning: establishing an effective and a stable Islamic Movement led by the Muslim Brotherhood which adopts Muslims' causes domestically and globally, and which works to expand the observant Muslim base, aims at unifying and directing Muslims' efforts, presents Islam as a civilization alternative, and supports the global Islamic State wherever it is." 2- The priority that is approved by the Shura Council for the work of the Group in its current and former session which is "Settlement." 3- The positive development with the brothers in the Islamic Circle in an attempt to reach a unity of merger. 4- The constant need for thinking and future planning, an attempt to read it and working to 'shape' the present to comply and suit the needs and challenges of the future. 5- The paper of his eminence, the General Masul, may God keep him, which he recently sent to the members of the Council.

Two: An Introduction to the Explanatory Memorandum:

In order to begin with the explanation, we must "summon" the following question and place it in front of our eyes as its relationship is important and necessary with the strategic goal and the explanation project we are embarking on. The question we are facing is: "How do you like to see the Islam Movement in North America in ten years?", or "taking along" the following sentence when planning and working, "Islamic Work in North America in the year (2000): A Strategic Vision."

Also, we must summon and take along "elements" of the general strategic goal of the Group in North America and I will intentionally repeat them in numbers. They are:

1- Establishing an effective and stable Islamic Movement led by the Muslim Brotherhood. 2- Adopting Muslims' causes domestically and globally. 3- Expanding the observant Muslim base. 4- Unifying and directing Muslims' efforts. 5- Presenting Islam as a civilization alternative. 6- Supporting the establishment of global Islamic State wherever it is.

It must be stressed that it has become clear and emphatically known that all is in agreement that we must "settle" or "enable" Islam and its Movement in this part of the world. Therefore, a joint understanding of the meaning of settlement or enablement must be adopted, through which and on whose basis we explain the general strategic goal with its six elements for the Group in North America.

Three: The Concept of Settlement:

This term was mentioned in the Group's "dictionary" and documents with various meanings in spite of the fact that everyone meant one

199

thing with it. We believe that the understanding of the essence is the same and we will attempt here to give the word and its "meanings" a practical explanation with a practical Movement tone, and not a philosophical linguistic explanation, while stressing that this explanation of ours is not complete until our explanation of "the process" of settlement itself is understood which is mentioned in the following paragraph. We briefly say the following:

Settlement: "That Islam and its Movement become a part of the homeland it lives in". Establishment: "That Islam turns into firmly-rooted organizations on whose bases civilization, structure and testimony are built". Stability: "That Islam is stable in the land on which its people move". Enablement: "That Islam is enabled within the souls, minds and the lives of the people of the country in which it moves". Rooting: "That Islam is resident and not a passing thing, or rooted "entrenched" in the soil of the spot where it moves and not a strange plant to it".

Four : The Process of Settlement:

In order for Islam and its Movement to become "a part of the homeland" in which it lives, "stable" in its land, "rooted" in the spirits and minds of its people, "enabled" in the live of its society and has firmly-established "organizations" on which the Islamic structure is built and with which the testimony of civilization is achieved, the Movement must plan and struggle to obtain "the keys" and the tools of this process in carry out this grand mission as a "Civilization Jihadist" responsibility which lies on the shoulders of Muslims and - on top of them - the Muslim Brotherhood in this country. Among these keys and tools are the following:

1- Adopting the concept of settlement and understanding its practical meanings: The Explanatory Memorandum focused on the Movement and the realistic dimension of the process of settlement and its practical meanings without paying attention to the difference in understanding between the resident and the non-resident, or who is the settled and the non-settled and we believe that what was mentioned in the long-term plan in that regards suffices.

2- Making a fundamental shift in our thinking and mentality in order to suit the challenges of the settlement mission: What is meant with the shift - which is a positive expression - is responding to the grand challenges of the settlement issues. We believe that any transforming response begins with the method of thinking and its center, the brain, first. In order to clarify what is meant with the shift as a key to qualify us to enter the field of settlement, we say very briefly that the following must be accomplished:

A shift from the partial thinking mentality to the comprehensive thinking mentality.

A shift from the "amputated" partial thinking mentality to the "continuous" comprehensive mentality.

A shift from the mentality of caution and reservation to the mentality of risk and controlled liberation.

A shift from the mentality of the elite Movement to the mentality of the popular Movement.

A shift from the mentality of preaching and guidance to the mentality of building and testimony.

A shift from the single opinion mentality to the multiple opinion mentality.

A shift from the collision mentality to the absorption mentality.

A shift from the individual mentality to the team mentality.

A shift from the anticipation mentality to the initiative mentality.

A shift from the hesitation mentality to the decisiveness mentality.

A shift from the principles mentality to the programs mentality.

A shift from the abstract ideas mentality the true organizations mentality [This is the core point and the essence of the memorandum].

3- Understanding the historical stages in which the Islamic Ikhwani activism went through in this country: The writer of the memorandum believes that understanding and comprehending the historical stages of the Islamic activism which was led and being led by the Muslim Brotherhood in this continent is a very important key in working towards settlement, through which the Group observes its march, the direction of its movement and the curves and turns of its road. We will suffice here with mentioning the title for each of these stages [The title expresses the prevalent characteristic of the stage] [Details maybe mentioned in another future study]. Most likely, the stages are:

A- The stage of searching for self and determining the identity.
B- The stage of inner build-up and tightening the organization.
C- The stage of mosques and the Islamic centers.
D- The stage of building the Islamic organizations - the first phase.
E- The stage of building the Islamic schools - the first phase.
F- The stage of thinking about the overt Islamic Movement - the first phase.
G- The stage of openness to the other Islamic movements and attempting to reach a formula for dealing with them - the first phase.
H- The stage of reviving and establishing the Islamic organizations - the second phase.

We believe that the Group is embarking on this stage in its second phase as it has to open the door and enter as it did the first time.

4-Understanding the role of the Muslim Brother in North America: The process of settlement is a "Civilization-Jihadist Process" with all the word means. The Ikhwan must understand that their work in America is a kind of grand Jihad in eliminating and destroying the Western civilization from within and "sabotaging" its miserable house by their hands and the hands of the believers so that it is eliminated and God's religion is made victorious over all other religions. Without this level of understanding, we are not up to this challenge and have not prepared ourselves for Jihad yet. It is a Muslim's destiny to perform Jihad and work wherever he is and wherever he lands until the final hour comes, and there is no escape from that destiny except for those who chose to slack. But, would the slackers and the Mujahedeen be equal.

5-Understanding that we cannot perform the settlement mission by ourselves or away from people: A mission as significant and as huge as the settlement mission needs magnificent and exhausting efforts. With their capabilities, human, financial and scientific resources, the Ikhwan will not be able to carry out this mission alone or away from people and he who believes that is wrong, and God knows best. As for the role of the Ikhwan, it is the initiative, pioneering, leadership, raising the banner and pushing people in that direction. They are then to work to employ, direct and unify Muslims' efforts and powers for this process. In order to do that, we must possess a mastery of the art of "coalitions", the art of "absorption" and the principles of "cooperation".

6-The necessity of achieving a union and balanced gradual merger between private work and public work: We believe that what was written about this subject is many and is enough. But, it needs a time and a practical frame so that what is needed is achieved in a gradual and a balanced way that is compatible with the process of settlement.

7-The conviction that the success of the settlement of Islam and its Movement in this country is a success to the global Islamic Movement and a true support for the sought-after state, God willing: There is a conviction - with which this memorandum disagrees - that our focus in attempting to settle Islam in this country will lead to negligence in our duty towards the global Islamic Movement in supporting its project to establish the state. We believe that the reply is in two segments: One - The success of the Movement in America in establishing an observant Islamic base with power and effectiveness will be the best support and aid to the global Movement project. And the second - is the global Movement has not succeeded yet in "distributing roles" to its branches, stating what is the needed from them as one of the participants or contributors to the project to establish the global Islamic state. The day this happens, the children of the American Ikhwani branch will have far-reaching impact and positions that make the ancestors proud.

8-Absorbing Muslims and winning them with all of their factions and colors in America and Canada for the settlement project, and making it their cause, future and the basis of their Islamic life in this part of the world: This issues requires from us to learn "the art of dealing with the others", as people are different and people in many colors. We need to adopt the principle which says, "Take from people... the best they have", their best specializations, experiences, arts, energies and abilities. By people here we mean those within or without the ranks of individuals and organizations. The policy of "taking" should be with what achieves the strategic goal and the settlement process. But the big challenge in front of us is: how to connect them all in "the orbit" of our plan and "the circle" of our Movement in order to achieve "the core" of our interest. To me, there is no choice for us other than alliance and mutual understanding of those who desire from our religion and those who agree from our belief in work. And the U.S. Islamic arena is full of those waiting...., the pioneers.

What matters is bringing people to the level of comprehension of the challenge that is facing us as Muslims in this country, conviction of our settlement project, and understanding the benefit of agreement, cooperation and alliance. At that time, if we ask for money, a lot of it would come, and if we ask for men, they would come in lines. What matters is that our plan is "the criterion and the balance" in our relationship with others.

Here, two points must be noted; the first one: we need to comprehend and understand the balance of the Islamic powers in the U.S. arena [and this might be the subject of a future study]. The second point: what we reached with the brothers in "ICNA" is considered a step in the right direction, the beginning of good and the first drop that requires growing and guidance.

9-Re-examining our organizational and administrative bodies, the type of leadership and the method of selecting it with what suits the challenges of the settlement mission: The memorandum will be silent about details regarding this item even though it is logical and there is a lot to be said about it,

10-Growing and developing our resources and capabilities, our financial and human resources with what suits the magnitude of the grand mission: If we examined the human and the financial resources the Ikhwan alone own in this country, we and others would feel proud and glorious. And if we add to them the resources of our friends and allies, those who circle in our orbit and those waiting on our banner, we would realize that we are able to open the door to settlement and walk through it seeking to make Almighty God's word the highest.

11-Utilizing the scientific method in planning, thinking and preparation of studies needed for the process of settlement:
Yes, we need this method, and we need many studies which aid in this civilization Jihadist operation. We will mention some of them

briefly:

The history of the Islamic presence in America.
The history of the Islamic Ikhwani presence in America.
Islamic movements, organizations and organizations: analysis and criticism.
The phenomenon of the Islamic centers and schools: challenges, needs and statistics.
Islamic minorities,
Muslim and Arab communities.
The U.S. society: make-up and politics.
The U.S. society's view of Islam and Muslims... And many other studies which we can direct our brothers and allies to prepare, either through their academic studies or through their educational centers or organizational tasking. What is important is that we start.

12-Agreeing on a flexible, balanced and a clear "mechanism" to implement the process of settlement within a specific, gradual and balanced "time frame" that is in-line with the demands and challenges of the process of settlement.

13-Understanding the U.S. society from its different aspects an understanding that "qualifies" us to perform the mission of settling our Dawa' in its country "and growing it" on its land.

14-Adopting a written "jurisprudence" that includes legal and movement bases, principles, policies and interpretations which are suitable for the needs and challenges of the process of settlement.

15-Agreeing on "criteria" and balances to be a sort of "antennas" or "the watch tower" in order to make sure that all of our priorities, plans, programs, bodies, leadership, monies and activities march towards the process of the settlement.

16-Adopting a practical, flexible formula through which our central

work complements our domestic work.
[Items 12 through 16 will be detailed later].

17-Understanding the role and the nature of work of "The Islamic Center" in every city with what achieves the goal of the process of settlement: The center we seek is the one which constitutes the "axis" of our Movement, the "perimeter" of the circle of our work, our "balance center", the "base" for our rise and our "Dar al-Arqam" to educate us, prepare us and supply our battalions in addition to being the "niche" of our prayers.

This is in order for the Islamic center to turn - in action not in words - into a seed "for a small Islamic society" which is a reflection and a mirror to our central organizations. The center ought to turn into a "beehive" which produces sweet honey. Thus, the Islamic center would turn into a place for study, family, battalion, course, seminar, visit, sport, school, social club, women gathering, kindergarten for male and female youngsters, the office of the domestic political resolution, and the center for distributing our newspapers, magazines, books and our audio and visual tapes.

In brief we say: we would like for the Islamic center to become "The House of Dawa'" and "the general center" in deeds first before name. As much as we own and direct these centers at the continent level, we can say we are marching successfully towards the settlement of Dawa' in this country.

Meaning that the "center's" role should be the same as the "mosque's" role during the time of God's prophet, God's prayers and peace be upon him, when he marched to "settle" the Dawa' in its first generation in Madina. from the mosque, he drew the Islamic life and provided to the world the most magnificent and fabulous civilization humanity knew.

This mandates that, eventually, the region, the branch and the Usra turn into "operations rooms" for planning, direction, monitoring and leadership for the Islamic center in order to be a role model to be followed.

18-Adopting a system that is based on "selecting" workers, "role distribution" and "assigning" positions and responsibilities is based on specialization, desire and need with what achieves the process of settlement and contributes to its success.

19-Turning the principle of dedication for the Masuls of main positions within the Group into a rule, a basis and a policy in work. Without it, the process of settlement might be stalled [Talking about this point requires more details and discussion].

20-Understanding the importance of the "Organizational" shift in our Movement work, and doing Jihad in order to achieve it in the real world with what serves the process of settlement and expedites its results, God Almighty's willing: The reason this paragraph was delayed is to stress its utmost importance as it constitutes the heart and the core of this memorandum. It also constitutes the practical aspect and the true measure of our success or failure in our march towards settlement. The talk about the organizations and the "organizational" mentality or phenomenon does not require much details. It suffices to say that the first pioneer of this phenomenon was our prophet Mohamed, God's peace, mercy and blessings be upon him, as he placed the foundation for the first civilized organization which is the mosque, which truly became "the comprehensive organization". And this was done by the pioneer of the contemporary Islamic Dawa', Imam martyr Hasan al-Banna, may God have mercy on him, when he and his brothers felt the need to "re-establish" Islam and its movement anew, leading him to establish organizations with all their kinds: economic, social, media, scouting, professional and even the military ones. We must say that we are in a country which understands no language other than the language of the organizations, and one which does not respect or give weight to any group without effective, functional and strong organizations.

It is good fortune that there are brothers among us who have this "trend", mentality or inclination to build the organizations who have beat us by action and words which leads us to dare say honestly what Sadat in Egypt once said, "We want to build a country of organizations" - a word of right he meant wrong with. I say to my brothers, let us raise the banner of truth to establish right "We want to establish the Group of organizations", as without it we will not able to put our feet on the true path.

And in order for the process of settlement to be completed, we must plan and work from now to equip and prepare ourselves, our brothers, our apparatuses, our sections and our committees in order to turn into comprehensive organizations in a gradual and balanced way that is suitable with the need and the reality. What encourages us to do that - in addition to the aforementioned -is that we possess "seeds" for each organization from the organization we call for.
All we need is to tweak them, coordinate their work, collect their elements and merge their efforts with others and then connect them with the comprehensive plan we seek.

For instance, We have a seed for a "comprehensive media and art" organization: we own a print + advanced typesetting machine + audio and visual center + art production office + magazines in Arabic and English [The Horizons, The Hope, The Politicians, Ha Falastine, Press Clips, al-Zaytouna, Palestine Monitor, Social Sciences Magazines...] + art band + photographers + producers + programs anchors + journalists + in addition to other media and art experiences". Another example:

We have a seed for a "comprehensive Dawa' educational" organization: We have the Daw'a section in ISNA + Dr. Jamal Badawi Foundation + the center run by brother Hamed al-Ghazali +

the Dawa' center the Dawa' Committee and brother Shaker al-Sayyed are seeking to establish now + in addition to other Daw'a efforts here and there...". And this applies to all the organizations we call on establishing.

The big challenge that is ahead of us is how to turn these seeds or "scattered" elements into comprehensive, stable, "settled" organizations that are connected with our Movement and which fly in our orbit and take orders from our guidance. This does not prevent - but calls for - each central organization to have its local branches but its connection with the Islamic center in the city is a must.

What is needed is to seek to prepare the atmosphere and the means to achieve "the merger" so that the sections, the committees, the regions, the branches and the Usras are eventually the heart and the core of these organizations. Or, for the shift and the change to occur as follows:

1- The Movement Department + The Secretariat Department
2- Education Department + Dawa'a Com.
3- Sisters Department
4- The Financial Department + Investment Committee + The Endowment
5- Youth Department + Youths Organizations Department
6- The Social Committee + Matrimony Committee + Mercy Foundation
7- The Security Committee
8- The Political Depart. + Palestine Com.
9- The Group's Court + The Legal Com.
10-Domestic Work Department
11- Our magazines + the print + our art band
12- The Studies Association + The Publication House + Dar al-Kitab
13- Scientific and Medial societies
14- The Organizational Conference

15- The Shura Council + Planning Com.
16- The Executive Office
17- The General Masul
18- The regions, branches & Usras

The Organizational & Administrative Organization -The General Center
Dawa' and Educational Organization
The Women's Organization
The Economic Organization
Youth Organizations
The Social Organization
The Security Organization
The Political Organization
The Judicial Organization
Its work is to be distributed to the rest of the organizations
The Media and Art Organization
The Intellectual & Cultural Organization
Scientific, Educational & Professional Organization
The Islamic-American Founding Conference
The Shura Council for the Islamic-American Movement
The Executive Office of the Islamic-American Movement
Chairman of the Islamic Movement and its official Spokesman
Field leaders of organizations & Islamic centers

Five: Comprehensive Settlement Organization:
We would then seek and struggle in order to make each one of these above-mentioned organizations a "comprehensive organization" throughout the days and the years, and as long as we are destined to be in this country. What is important is that we put the foundation and we will be followed by peoples and generations that would finish the march and the road but with a clearly-defined guidance.

And, in order for us to clarify what we mean with the comprehensive, specialized organization, we mention here the characteristics and traits of each organization of the "promising" organizations.

1-From the Dawa' and educational aspect [The Dawa* and Educational Organization]: to include:

The Organization to spread the Dawa' (Central and local branches).
An institute to graduate Callers and Educators.
Scholars, Callers, Educators, Preachers and Program Anchors.
Art and communication technology, Conveyance and Dawa'.
A television station.
A specialized Dawa' magazine.
A radio station.
The Higher Islamic Council for Callers and Educators.
The Higher Council for Mosques and Islamic Centers.
Friendship Societies with the other religions... and things like that.

2-Politically [The Political Organization]: to include:

A central political party.
Local political offices.
Political symbols.
Relationships and alliances.
The American Organization for Islamic Political Action
Advanced Information Centers....and things like that.

3-Media [The Media and Art Organization]: to include:

A daily newspaper,
Weekly, monthly and seasonal magazines.
Radio stations.
Television programs.
Audio and visual centers.
A magazine for the Muslim child.
A magazine for the Muslim woman.
A print and typesetting machines.

A production office.
A photography and recording studio
Art bands for acting, chanting and theater.
A marketing and art production office... and things like that.

4-Economically [The Economic Organization!: to include:

An Islamic Central bank.
Islamic endowments.
Investment projects.
An organization for interest-free loans.... and things like that.

5-Scientifically and Professionally [The Scientific. Educational and Professional Organization]: to include:

Scientific research centers.
Technical organizations and vocational training.
An Islamic university.
Islamic schools.
A council for education and scientific research.
Centers to train teachers.
Scientific societies in schools.
An office for academic guidance.
A body for authorship and Islamic curricula.... and things like that.

6-Culturally and Intellectually [The Cultural and Intellectual Organization]: to include:

A center for studies and research.
Cultural and intellectual foundations such as [The Social Scientists Society - Scientists and Engineers Society....].
An organization for Islamic thought and culture.
A publication, translation and distribution house for Islamic books.

An office for archiving, history and authentication
The project to translate the Noble Quran, the Noble Sayings....and things like that.

7-Socially [The Social-Charitable Organization]: to include:

Social clubs for the youths and the community's sons and daughters
Local societies for social welfare and the services are tied to the Islamic centers
The Islamic Organization to Combat the Social Ills of the U.S. Society
Islamic houses project
Matrimony and family cases office....and things like that.

8-Youths [The Youth Organization!: to include:

Central and local youths foundations.
Sports teams and clubs
Scouting teams....and things like that.

9-Women [The Women Organization]: to include:

Central and local women societies.
Organizations of training, vocational and housekeeping.
An organization to train female preachers.
Islamic kindergartens...and things like that.

10-Organizationally and Administratively [The Administrative and Organizational Organization!: to include:

An institute for training, growth, development and planning
Prominent experts in this field
Work systems, bylaws and charters fit for running the most complicated bodies and organizations

A periodic magazine in Islamic development and administration.
Owning camps and halls for the various activities.
A data, polling and census bank.
An advanced communication network.
An advanced archive for our heritage and production....and things like that.

11-Security [The Security Organization!: to include:

Clubs for training and learning self-defense techniques.
A center which is concerned with the security issues [Technical, intellectual, technological and human]....and things like that.

12-Legally [The Legal Organization]: to include:

A Central Jurisprudence Council.
A Central Islamic Court.
Muslim Attorneys Society.
The Islamic Foundation for Defense of Muslims' Rights...and things like that. And success is by God.

Attachment

A list of our organizations and the organizations of our friends (Imagine if they all march according to one plan!!!)

ISNA   ISAMIC SOCIETY OF NORTH AMERICA
MSA   MUSLIM STUDENT'S ASSOCIATION
MCA   THE MUSLIM COMMUNITIES ASSOCIATION
AMSS   THE ASSOCIATION OF MUSLIM SOCIAL SCIENTISTS
AMSE   THE ASSN OF MUSLIM SCIENTISTS AND ENGINEERS
IMA   ISLAMIC MEDICAL ASSOCIATION
ITC   ISLAMIC TEACHING CENTER
NAIT   NORTH AMERICAN ISLAMIC TRUST
FID   FOUNDATION FOR INTERNATIONAL DEVELOPMENT

IHC   ISLAMIC HOUSING COOPERATIVE
ICD   ISLAMIC CENTERS DIVIDION
ATP   AMERICAN TRUST PUBLICATIONS
AVC   AUDIO-VISUAL CENTER
IBS   ISLAMIC BOOK SERVICE
MBA   MUSLIM BUSINESSMEN ASSOCIATION
MYNA   MUSLIM YOUTH OF NORTH AMERICA
IFC   ISNA FIQH COMMITTEE
IPAC   ISNA POLITICAL AWARENESS COMMITTEE
IED   ISLAMIC EDUCATION DEPARTMENT
MAYA   MUSLIM ARAB YOUTH ASSOCIATION
MISG   MALASIAN ISLAMIC STUDY GROUP
IAP   ISLAMIC ASSOCIATION FOR PALESTINE
UASR   UNITED ASSOCIATION FOR STUDIES AND RESEARCH
OLF   OCCUPIED LAND FUND
MIA   MERCY INTERNATIONAL ASSOCIATION
ICNA   ISLAMIC CIRCLE OF NORTH AMERICA
BMI   BAITUL MAL INC
IIIT   INTERNAIONAL INSTITUTE FOR ISLAMIC THOUGHT
IIC   ISLAMIC INFORMATION CENTER
CAIR   COUNCIL ON AMERICAN-ISLAMIC RELATIONS

This is the Islamic plan for their 'silent Jihad.' It's already well-advanced in our nation. And, too many are turning their backs and closing their eyes; and closing their ears not to see it, hear it, or understand it. Our national leaders are not only refusing to challenge this silent Jihad, they seem to be encouraging it and supporting it.

This is the infiltration plan by the 'peaceful' Muslims while their more radical Muslim brothers distract us with their gun, swords, and endless threats. A devious and Satanic plan; that's working for them as our government refuses to do anything to stop them.

Although it's a silent Jihad, it's more dangerous and effective against our democracy and freedom than is their terrorist approach. The terror head of the two-headed snake is the distraction; while the silent part of the two-headed snake silently wraps its body in a death grip around our freedom. That deadly snake, Satan, is already closer than one can imagine.

To summarize that document, it gives long and detailed instructions regarding every part of our American society. It covers infiltration into the arts and sciences, education, social clubs, social networking, and any other place one can imagine squeezing into to create a footprint that can later be used to bring the whole Muslim Brotherhood project together. In short, it suggests to 'be nice' and participate, then when the stage is set to begin taking more control over that particular area. Where are our leaders; who are sworn to protect us and the United States of America? Are they for us or against us? Their actions and words are not comforting toward that goal.

217

Chapter 13
Safety and Security

O
ur current administration under Barack Obama seems not only to be cooperating with that Muslim Memorandum plan, but also appears in many ways to be part of the plan itself. The Muslim Brotherhood has already worked itself into a strong foothold in the federal administration as well as into our education systems. Obama paves the way for them to advance. He has appointed many to very high and influential positions. A simple research online shows who they are.

Defending America

The first responsibility of a President of the United States is to protect the citizens of the United States. That's the fundamental purpose of a president; not to create welfare, and not to put some citizens in more favored positions than other citizens. Now, to fulfill that goal, it would seem the interest of the president would lie with the interests and concerns of the citizenry. From Barack Obama's actions and comments, can one determine where his loyalties and intentions are?

Are they with the American citizens long guided by Judeo-Christian principles, or are they framed by total commitment to one occupying only a remnant position to that long-standing American culture of freedom and democracy? Let's examine the history of his actions and words to determine if a biased loyalty might exist that's not in great favor to the loyalties expected as one leading our great nation. In large part, let's listen to his own words about his intentions and biases. The first question concerns his real and true religion. These must be examined seriously and deeply; for his intentions and actions greatly affect the security of our nation, and the safety and security of every single citizen of our great nation.

This next article is from Conservapedia.com, titled: 'Obama's Religion.' The article contains references at the end of each sub article that may be identified and cross-referenced by searching the article and source online. They are deleted here to facilitate easier reading. The information in this article is important in reference to Revelation 17: 8 and 11. This is the article:

"Public opinion polls show that despite liberal denial, at least one in five or 17% of Americans recognize that Barack Hussein Obama is a Muslim. While campaigning for president in 2008, Obama claimed to be a Christian in an interview he gave to Christianity Today magazine:

"I am a Christian, and I am a devout Christian. I believe in the redemptive death and resurrection of Jesus Christ. I believe that that faith gives me a path to be cleansed of sin and have eternal life. But most importantly, I believe in the example that Jesus set by feeding the hungry and healing the sick and always prioritizing the least of these over the powerful. I didn't 'fall out in church' as they say, but there was a very strong awakening in me of the importance of these issues in my life. I didn't want to walk alone on this journey. Accepting Jesus Christ in my life has been a powerful guide for my conduct and my values and my ideals.

There is one thing that I want to mention that I think is important.

Part of what we've been seeing during the course of this campaign is some scurrilous e-mails that have been sent out, denying my faith, talking about me being a Muslim, suggesting that I got sworn in at the U.S. Senate with a Quran in my hand or that I don't pledge allegiance to the flag. I think it's really important for your readers to know that I have been a member of the same church for almost 20 years, and I have never practiced Islam. I am respectful of the religion, but it's not my own. One of the things that's very important in this day and age is that we don't use religion as a political tool and certainly that we don't lie about religion as a way to score political points. I just thought it was important to get that in there to dispel rumors that have been over the Internet. We've done so repeatedly, but obviously it's a political tactic of somebody to try to provide this misinformation."

Of course, what politicians claim while campaigning for an election, and what the truth is, are often two different things. Historians look at all the evidence, not merely what a politician campaigning for office says. The following is a list of evidence indicating that Obama is a Muslim:

Obama declared in prepared remarks, "The United States has been enriched by Muslim Americans. Many other Americans have Muslims in their families or have lived in a Muslim-majority country - I know, because I am one of them."

Obama's wife Michelle does not accompany him to Muslim nations because Sharia law would require her to wear a head covering as the wife of a Muslim man in a Muslim nation; on a presidential trip she was with him until France, but then returned home.

In prepared remarks in April 2012, Obama referred to Jesus as "a" Son of God rather than as "the" Son of God: "And for me, and I'm sure for some of you, it's also a chance to remember the tremendous sacrifice that led up to that day, and all that Christ endured—not just as a Son of God, but as a human being."

Obama's background and outlook are Muslim, and fewer than 1% of Muslims convert to Christianity. Although Obama attended a Catholic school while in Indonesia, he was a part of the Muslim society there.

Obama's middle name (Hussein) references Husayn, who was the grandson of Muhammad. Only after Obama became politically ambitious did he declare himself to be a Christian, yet he never replaced his Muslim name "Hussein" with a Christian one as some do when they undergo a religious conversion. For example, when the Italian journalist Magdi Allam recently converted to Christianity, he took a new name: "Cristiano". When Saul became a Christian, he changed his name to "Paul"; when the famous boxer Cassius Clay converted to Islam, he took the Muslim name of Muhammad Ali. "It is common for those converting to a new religion to change their name on conversion" or adopt a Christian name at baptism. Obama also used his middle name when sworn in as President. However, even if he were actually a Muslim, he would not necessarily have to change his name according to Muslim tradition.

Obama said that "John McCain has not talked about my Muslim faith," in an interview with George Stephanopoulos discussing whether John McCain's campaign has suggested that Obama is not a Christian. George Stephanopoulos -- who had previously been a high-ranking Democrat in the Clinton Administration -- then suggested that Obama change his answer to refer instead to "Christian faith."

He has said that "Islam can be compatible with the modern world."

Obama said the Muslim call to prayer is "one of the prettiest sounds on Earth at sunset," and recited "with a first-class Arabic accent" the opening lines: Allah is Supreme! ... I witness that there is no god but

Allah ...."

Obama's unusual selection of Chuck Hagel, a former Republican senator most sympathetic to Muslim positions in the Middle East, to be Secretary of Defense despite intense objections by both political parties. Iranian State Press approves of the choice.

Obama seems to emotionally hold a Muslim view about Israel, in contrast with Americans who have been educated as Obama has. Obama never visited Israel during his first term as president despite repeated criticisms of his failure to do so, he oddly waited many days before even mentioning the rocket attacks on Israel in late 2012, and he appears very uncomfortable even discussing issues related to Israel on television.

Liberals at the New York Times and the Huffington Post fawn over the Indonesian ring that Obama has worn since long before his marriage to Michelle Obama. It has been reported that this ring has Islamic inscriptions. (Note: I recently published a book titled, 'Obama's Ring: The Seat of Satan.' In that book, I disputed the allegation that the ring contained Islamic inscriptions. Instead, the ring contains icons of two coiled serpents - the serpent being the representation of Satan used throughout the Bible. A close-up photograph of the ring can be seen online by searching, 'Obama's Ring.')

Obama stated that the Autobiography of Malcolm X, which was co-written by Alex Haley, inspired him in his youth.

Obama raised nearly $1 million and campaigned for a Kenyan presidential candidate who had a written agreement with Muslim leaders promising to convert Kenya to an Islamic state that bans Christianity.

Obama's claims of conversion to Christianity arose after he became politically ambitious, lacking a date of conversion or baptism.

In 2007, while Obama was a candidate, the White House military office assigned him the Secret Service code name "Renegade". "Renegade" conventionally describes someone who goes against normal conventions of behavior, but its first usage was to describe someone who has turned from their religion. It is a word derived from the Spanish renegado, which originally meant "Christian turned Muslim." In the book Obama,"Renegade" his friends say that "he actually really wasn't much of a churchgoer."

On the 2008 campaign trail, Obama was reading "The Post-American World" by Fareed Zakaria, which was a general discussion of US foreign policy that was on the non-fiction best-seller lists for weeks. Although Zakaria had Muslim ancestors, he is a non-Muslim educated at Yale with a Ph.D. from Harvard.

Contrary to Christianity, the Islamic doctrine of taqiyya allows adherents to deny they are Muslim if it would be dangerous not to.

Obama uses the Muslim Pakistani pronunciation for "Pakistan" rather than the common American one. Obama favors Pakistan, a Muslim nation, in its conflicts with India, a mostly Hindu nation. However, the Obama Administration's relationship with Pakistan could be driven by its critical role in the battle against al-Qaeda in Afghanistan.

Obama was thoroughly exposed to Christianity as an adult in Chicago prior to attending law school, yet no one at law school saw him display any interest in converting. Obama unabashedly explained how he became "churched" in a 2007 speech: "It's around that time [while working as an organizer for the Developing Communities Project (DCP) of the Calumet Community Religious Conference (CCRC) in Chicago] that some pastors I was working with came around and asked if I was a member of a church. 'If you're organizing churches,' they said, 'it might be helpful if you went to a church once in a while.' And I thought, 'I guess that makes sense.'"

"I really endorse and support the policies that he has adopted," Libyan leader Muammar Gaddafi said of President Barack Obama as reported by the Washington Post.

Obama is mentioned as helping to organize the 1995 Million Man March led by black Muslim leader Louis Farrakhan from the Nation of Islam.

Obama visited "more than one mosque" in Kenya while on a political trip there but did not visit any churches, although there are a large proportion of churches and even a National Temple in Kenya.

Obama enjoyed a bigger increase in voter support in 2008 (compared to 2004) by Muslims than by any other voting group, including blacks; "Muslim turnout in the U.S. elections reached 95 percent, the highest Muslim turnout in U.S. history."

Obama rarely attends church or has church services in the White House. "President-elect Barack Hussein Obama has yet to attend [Sunday] church services since winning the White House earlier ..., a departure from the example of his two immediate predecessors."

In 2009, Justice John Roberts failed to administer the oath of office correctly while Obama placed his hand on a Bible. To avoid any claims that Obama was not the real President because of mis-stating the oath, Roberts dropped by the White House to re-administering the oath the next day, but no Bible was used for that private re-do of the oath.

At the G-20 summit in April 2009, Obama bowed deeply to Saudi King Abdullah, a Muslim who is also the Custodian of the Two Holy Mosques.

President Obama bowing to the King of Saudi Arabia - April 2009: Never before in the history of the U.S. has a president displayed such shocking deference to a foreign official and Obama has not bowed to any other royal leaders. Obama later stated, "We have to change our behavior in showing the Muslim world greater respect." Obama's spin doctors and left-wing apologists dismissed the obviousness of the bow. One anonymous aide stated, "It wasn't a bow. He grasped his hand with two hands, and he's taller than King Abdullah." However, in video of the incident, Obama's left hand can clearly be seen staying at his side until after he had finished his bow. Additionally, Obama also met with Queen Elizabeth, who is much shorter than King Abdullah, but he did not bow when he shook her hand and neither he nor the queen appeared to have any difficulty. (Many liberals and even a handful of conservatives have proposed that President Bush also bowed before King Abdullah. However, there is a vast, inexorable difference between bending down to receive a medal as Bush did and bowing in deference to a foreign leader as Obama did.)

Obama required that a religiously affiliated college take the extraordinary action of concealing with wood the monogram "IHS", which represents the name of Jesus, during a speech by Obama there.

In 2006, Obama gave an irreverent speech about using the Bible in public policy. It resembled a stand-up comedy act, with Obama making fun of the books of the Torah, the Ten Commandments, the Sermon on the Mount and other key Biblical passages.

In 2010, while Obama was president, the Missile Defense Agency changed its logo, incorporating a crescent and star. The new logo closely resembles that of the Iranian Space Agency. The new logo was designed in 2007, prior to Obama's election as president.

In 2012, Obama participated in a $40,000 per plate fundraiser on Holy Thursday, which many devout Christians would find to be inappropriate.

On September 25, 2012, in his address to United Nations General Assembly, Obama said that "The future must not belong to those who slander the prophet of Islam." This outrageous comment was predictably ignored by the lamestream media, but rightly highlighted by Conservative commentators.

Obama's spiritual mentor of 20 years, Rev. Jeremiah Wright explained in an interview "that Barack Obama was steeped in Islam when he first met him," and said he "made it comfortable" for Obama to accept Christianity without having renounce his Islamic background.

Obamacare has a provision enabling groups that have a religious objection to the individual mandate and who have forfeited the benefits of Social Security (such as the Amish) to claim a religious conscience opt-out of the individual mandate. Muslims would not be eligible for a religious exemption from the individual mandate, although other online commentators speculate that Muslims would be eligible for a religious exemption.

Obama further impedes the Christian faith on gay rights, telling military chaplains a statutory provision that would allow military chaplains to opt-out of performing gay marriages is "unnecessary and ill-advised," but he signed the bill into law anyway.

On more than one occasion, Obama verbally attacks the economic livelihood of Las Vegas for unknown reasons, and Obama has also criticized state lotteries despite being heavily favored by most Democrats. The reason may be that gambling is forbidden in the Koran.

Obama tries to downplay his Islamic background by claiming that his Kenyan Muslim father was a "confirmed atheist" before Obama was born, but in fact less than 1% of Kenyans are atheists, agnostics, or non-religious. There is apparently no evidence of any Christian activities or local church participation by Obama while he was in Massachusetts from 1988 to 1991. Finally, Obama abruptly left his radical Christian church in Chicago in 2008, when it became politically controversial, without first finding another church to join. On April 7, 2009, Obama toured a mosque in Istanbul, Turkey. End of article.

A Biblically-Hostile President

This is another article relating to Obama's religious tendencies. It was published by David Barton at Wallbuilders.com on April 30, 2014. It's titled: 'America's Most Biblically-Hostile U.S. President.' The related references to the data may be found with the online article:

"When one observes President Obama's unwillingness to accommodate America's four-century long religious conscience protection through his attempts to require Catholics to go against their own doctrines and beliefs, one is tempted to say that he is anti-Catholic. But that characterization would not be correct. Although he has recently singled out Catholics, he has equally targeted traditional Protestant beliefs over the past four years. So since he has attacked Catholics and Protestants, one is tempted to say that he is anti-Christian. But that, too, would be inaccurate.

He has been equally disrespectful in his appalling treatment of religious Jews in general and Israel in particular. So perhaps the most accurate description of his antipathy toward Catholics, Protestants, religious Jews, and the Jewish nation would be to characterize him as anti-Biblical. And then when his hostility toward Biblical people of faith is contrasted with his preferential treatment of Muslims and Muslim nations, it further strengthens the accuracy of the anti-

Biblical descriptor. In fact, there have been numerous clearly documented times when his pro-Islam positions have been the cause of his anti-Biblical actions.

Listed below in chronological order are (1) numerous records of his attacks on Biblical persons or organizations; (2) examples of the hostility toward Biblical faith that have become evident in the past three years in the Obama-led military; (3) a listing of his open attacks on Biblical values; and finally (4) a listing of numerous incidents of his preferential deference for Islam's activities and positions, including letting his Islamic advisors guide and influence his hostility toward people of Biblical faith. The bracketed number at the end of each item is the reference at the end of the article. (Find this at the online article.)

1. Acts of hostility toward people of Biblical faith:

December 2009-Present - The annual White House Christmas cards, rather than focusing on Christmas or faith, instead highlight things such as the family dogs. And the White House Christmas tree ornaments include figures such as Mao Tse-Tung and a drag queen.

June 2013 – The Obama Department of Justice defunds a Young Marines chapter in Louisiana because their oath mentioned God, and another youth program because it permits a voluntary student-led prayer.

February 2013 – The Obama Administration announces that the rights of religious conscience for individuals will not be protected under the Affordable Care Act.

January 2013 – Pastor Louie Giglio is pressured to remove himself from praying at the inauguration after it is discovered he once preached a sermon supporting the Biblical definition of marriage.

February 2012 – The Obama administration forgives student loans in exchange for public service, but announces it will no longer forgive student loans if the public service is related to religion.

January 2012 – The Obama administration argues that the First Amendment provides no protection for churches and synagogues in hiring their pastors and rabbis.

December 2011 – The Obama administration denigrates other countries' religious beliefs as an obstacle to radical homosexual rights.

November 2011 – President Obama opposes inclusion of President Franklin Roosevelt's famous D-Day Prayer in the WWII Memorial.

November 2011 – Unlike previous presidents, Obama studiously avoids any religious references in his Thanksgiving speech.

August 2011 – The Obama administration releases its new health care rules that override religious conscience protections for medical workers in the areas of abortion and contraception.

April 2011 – For the first time in American history, Obama urges passage of a non-discrimination law that does not contain hiring protections for religious groups, forcing religious organizations to hire according to federal mandates without regard to the dictates of their own faith, thus eliminating conscience protection in hiring.

February 2011 – Although he filled posts in the State Department, for more than two years Obama did not fill the post of religious freedom ambassador, an official that works against religious persecution across the world; he filled it only after heavy pressure from the public and from Congress.

January 2011 – After a federal law was passed to transfer a WWI

Memorial in the Mojave Desert to private ownership, the U. S. Supreme Court ruled that the cross in the memorial could continue to stand, but the Obama administration refused to allow the land to be transferred as required by law, and refused to allow the cross to be re-erected as ordered by the Court.

November 2010 – Obama misquotes the National Motto, saying it is "E pluribus unum" rather than "In God We Trust" as established by federal law.

October 19, 2010 – Obama begins deliberately omitting the phrase about "the Creator" when quoting the Declaration of Independence – an omission he has made on no less than seven occasions.

May 2009 – Obama declines to host services for the National Prayer Day (a day established by federal law) at the White House.

April 2009 – When speaking at Georgetown University, Obama orders that a monogram symbolizing Jesus' name be covered when he is making his speech.

April 2009 – In a deliberate act of disrespect, Obama nominated three pro-abortion ambassadors to the Vatican; of course, the pro-life Vatican rejected all three.

February 2009 – Obama announces plans to revoke conscience protection for health workers who refuse to participate in medical activities that go against their beliefs, and fully implements the plan in February 2011.

April 2008 – Obama speaks disrespectfully of Christians, saying they "cling to guns or religion" and have an "antipathy to people who aren't like them."

2. Acts of hostility from the Obama-led military toward people of Biblical faith:

December 2013 - A naval facility required that two nativity scenes -- scenes depicting the event that caused Christmas to be declared a national federal holiday -- be removed from the base dining hall and be confined to the base chapel, thus disallowing the open public acknowledgment of this national federal holiday.

December 2013 - An Air Force base that allowed various public displays ordered the removal of one simply because it contained religious content.

October 2013 – A counter-intelligence briefing at Fort Hood tells soldiers that evangelical Christians are a threat to Americans and that for a soldier to donate to such a group "was punishable under military regulations."

October 2013 – Catholic priests hired to serve as military chaplains are prohibited from performing Mass services at base chapels during the government financial shutdown. When they offered to freely do Mass for soldiers, without regard to whether or not the chaplains were receiving pay, they are still denied permission to do so.

October 2013 - The Air Force Academy, in response to a complaint from Mikey Weinstein's Military Religious Freedom Foundation, makes "so help me God" optional in cadets' honor oath.

August 2013 - A Department of Defense military training manual teaches soldiers that people who talk about "individual liberties, states' rights, and how to make the world a better place" are "extremists." It also lists the Founding Fathers -- those "colonists who sought to free themselves from British rule" -- as examples of those involved in "extremist ideologies and movements."

August 2013 - A Senior Master Sergeant was removed from his position and reassigned because he told his openly lesbian squadron commander that she should not punish a staff sergeant who expressed his views in favor of traditional marriage.

August 2013 - The military does not provide heterosexual couples specific paid leave to travel to a state just for the purpose of being married, but it did extend these benefits to homosexual couples who want to marry, thus giving them preferential treatment not available to heterosexuals.

August 2013 - The Air Force, in the midst of having launched a series of attacks against those expressing traditional religious or moral views, invited a drag queen group to perform at a base.

July 2013 - When an Air Force sergeant with years of military service questioned a same-sex marriage ceremony performed at the Air Force Academy's chapel, he received a letter of reprimand telling him that if he disagreed, he needed to get out of the military. His current six-year re-enlistment was then reduced to only one-year, with the notification that he "be prepared to retire at the end of this year."

July 2013 - An Air Force chaplain who posted a website article on the importance of faith and the origin of the phrase "There are no atheists in foxholes" was officially ordered to remove his post because some were offended by the use of that famous World War II phrase.

June 2013 - The U. S. Air Force, in consultation with the Pentagon, removed an inspirational painting that for years has been hanging at Mountain Home Air Force Base because its title was "Blessed Are The Peacemakers" -- a phrase from Matthew 5:9 in the Bible.

June 2013 – The Obama administration "strongly objects" to a Defense Authorization amendment to protect the constitutionally-guaranteed religious rights of soldiers and chaplains, claiming that it would have an "adverse effect on good order, discipline, morale, and mission accomplishment."

June 2013 – At a joint base in New Jersey, a video was made, based on a Super Bowl commercial, to honor First Sergeants. It stated: "On the eighth day, God looked down on His creation and said, 'I need someone who will take care of the Airmen.' So God created a First Sergeant." Because the video mentioned the word "God," the Air Force required that it be taken down.

June 2013 – An Army Master Sergeant is reprimanded, threatened with judicial action, and given a bad efficiency report, being told he was "no longer a team player," because he voiced his support of traditional marriage at his own promotion party.

May 2013 - The Pentagon announces that "Air Force members are free to express their personal religious beliefs as long as it does not make others uncomfortable. "Proselytizing (inducing someone to convert to one's faith) goes over that line," affirming if a sharing of faith makes someone feel uncomfortable that it could be a court-marital offense -- the military equivalent of a civil felony.

May 2013 - An Air Force officer was actually made to remove a personal Bible from his own desk because it "might" appear that he was condoning the particular religion to which he belonged.

April 2013 – Officials briefing U.S. Army soldiers placed "Evangelical Christianity" and "Catholicism" in a list that also included Al-Qaeda, Muslim Brotherhood, and Hamas as examples of "religious extremism."

April 2013 – The U.S. Army directs troops to scratch off and paint over tiny Scripture verse references that for decades had been forged into weapon scopes.

April 2013 - The Air Force creates a "religious tolerance" policy but consults only a militant atheist group to do so -- a group whose leader has described military personnel who are religious as 'spiritual rapists' and 'human monsters' and who also says that soldiers who proselytize are guilty of treason and sedition and should be punished to hold back a "tidal wave of fundamentalists."

January 2013 – President Obama announced his opposition to a provision in the 2013 National Defense Authorization Act protecting the rights of conscience for military chaplains.

June 2012 – Bibles for the American military have been printed in every conflict since the American Revolution, but the Obama Administration revokes the long-standing U. S. policy of allowing military service emblems to be placed on those military Bibles.

May 2012 – The Obama administration opposed legislation to protect the rights of conscience for military chaplains who do not wish to perform same-sex marriages in violation of their strongly-held religious beliefs.

April 2012 – A checklist for Air Force Inns will no longer include ensuring that a Bible is available in rooms for those who want to use them.

February 2012 – The U. S. Military Academy at West Point disinvites three star Army general and decorated war hero Lieutenant General William G. ("Jerry") Boykin (retired) from speaking at an event because he is an outspoken Christian.

February 2012 – The Air Force removes "God" from the patch of Rapid Capabilities Office (the word on the patch was in Latin: Dei).

February 2012 – The Army ordered Catholic chaplains not to read a letter to parishioners that their archbishop asked them to read.

November 2011 – The Air Force Academy rescinds support for Operation Christmas Child, a program to send holiday gifts to impoverished children across the world, because the program is run by a Christian charity.

November 2011 – President Obama opposes inclusion of President Franklin Roosevelt's famous D-Day Prayer in the WWII Memorial.

November 2011 – Even while restricting and disapprobating Christian religious expressions, the Air Force Academy pays $80,000 to add a Stonehenge-like worship center for pagans, druids, witches and Wiccans at the Air Force Academy.

September 2011 – Air Force Chief of Staff prohibits commanders from notifying airmen of programs and services available to them from chaplains.

September 2011 – The Army issues guidelines for Walter Reed Medical Center stipulating that "No religious items (i.e. Bibles, reading materials and/or facts) are allowed to be given away or used during a visit."

August 2011 – The Air Force stops teaching the Just War theory to officers in California because the course is taught by chaplains and is based on a philosophy introduced by St. Augustine in the third century AD – a theory long taught by civilized nations across the world (except now, America).

June 2011 – The Department of Veterans Affairs forbids references to God and Jesus during burial ceremonies at Houston National Cemetery.

January 2010 – Because of "concerns" raised by the Department of Defense, tiny Bible verse references that had appeared for decades on scopes and gunsights were removed.

3. Acts of hostility toward Biblical values:

March 2014 - The Obama administration seeks funding for every type of sex-education -- except that which reflects traditional moral values.

August 2013 - Non-profit charitable hospitals, especially faith-based ones, will face large fines or lose their tax-exempt status if they don't comply with new strangling paperwork requirements related to giving free treatment to poor clients who do not have Obamacare insurance coverage. Ironically, the first hospital in America was founded as a charitable institution in 1751 by Benjamin Franklin, and its logo was the Good Samaritan, with Luke 10:35 inscribed below him: "Take care of him, and I will repay thee," being designed specifically to offer free medical care to the poor. Benjamin Franklin's hospital would likely be fined unless he placed more resources and funds into paperwork rather than helping the poor under the new faith-hostile policy of the Obama administration.

August 2013 - USAID, a federal government agency, shut down a conference in South Korea the night before it was scheduled to take place because some of the presentations were not pro-abortion but instead presented information on abortion complications, including the problems of "preterm births, mental health issues, and maternal mortality" among women giving birth who had previous abortions.

June 2013 – The Obama Administration finalizes requirements that under the Obamacare insurance program, employers must make available abortion-causing drugs, regardless of the religious conscience objections of many employers and even despite the directive of several federal courts to protect the religious conscience of employers.

April 2013 – The United States Agency for Internal Development

(USAID), an official foreign policy agency of the U.S. government, begins a program to train homosexual activists in various countries around the world to overturn traditional marriage and anti-sodomy laws, targeting first those countries with strong Catholic influences, including Ecuador, Honduras, and Guatemala.

December 2012 – Despite having campaigned to recognize Jerusalem as Israel's capital, President Obama once again suspends the provisions of the Jerusalem Embassy Act of 1995 which requires the United States to recognize Jerusalem as the capital of Israel and to move the American Embassy there.

July 2012 - The Pentagon, for the first time, allows service members to wear their uniforms while marching in a parade - specifically, a gay pride parade in San Diego.

October 2011 – The Obama administration eliminates federal grants to the U.S. Conference of Catholic Bishops for their extensive programs that aid victims of human trafficking because the Catholic Church is anti-abortion.

September 2011 – The Pentagon directs that military chaplains may perform same-sex marriages at military facilities in violation of the federal Defense of Marriage Act.

July 2011 – Obama allows homosexuals to serve openly in the military, reversing a policy originally instituted by George Washington in March 1778.

March 2011 – The Obama administration refuses to investigate videos showing Planned Parenthood helping alleged sex traffickers get abortions for victimized underage girls.

February 2011 – Obama directs the Justice Department to stop defending the federal Defense of Marriage Act.

September 2010 – The Obama administration tells researchers to ignore a judge's decision striking down federal funding for embryonic stem cell research.

August 2010 – The Obama administration Cuts funding for 176 abstinence education programs.

July 2010 – The Obama administration uses federal funds in violation of federal law to get Kenya to change its constitution to include abortion.

September 16, 2009 – The Obama administration appoints as EEOC Commissioner Chai Feldblum, who asserts that society should "not tolerate" any "private beliefs," including religious beliefs, if they may negatively affect homosexual "equality."

July 2009 – The Obama administration illegally extends federal benefits to same-sex partners of Foreign Service and Executive Branch employees, in direction violation of the federal Defense of Marriage Act.

May 2009 – The White House budget eliminates all funding for abstinence-only education and replaces it with "comprehensive" sexual education, repeatedly proven to increase teen pregnancies and abortions. He continues the deletion in subsequent budgets.

May 2009 – Obama officials assemble a terrorism dictionary calling pro-life advocates violent and charging that they use racism in their "criminal" activities.

March 2009 – The Obama administration shut out pro-life groups from attending a White House-sponsored health care summit.

March 2009 – Obama orders taxpayer funding of embryonic stem cell research.

March 2009 – Obama gave $50 million for the UNFPA, the UN population agency that promotes abortion and works closely with Chinese population control officials who use forced abortions and involuntary sterilizations.

January 2009 – Obama lifts restrictions on U.S. government funding for groups that provide abortion services or counseling abroad, forcing taxpayers to fund pro-abortion groups that either promote or perform abortions in other nations.

January 2009 – President Obama's nominee for deputy secretary of state asserts that American taxpayers are required to pay for abortions and that limits on abortion funding are unconstitutional.

4. Acts of preferentialism for Islam:

February 2012 – The Obama administration makes effulgent apologies for Korans being burned by the U. S. military, but when Bibles were burned by the military, numerous reasons were offered why it was the right thing to do.

October 2011 – Obama's Muslim advisers block Middle Eastern Christians' access to the White House.

August 2010 – Obama speaks with great praise of Islam and condescendingly of Christianity.

August 2010 – Obama went to great lengths to speak out on multiple occasions on behalf of building an Islamic mosque at Ground Zero, while at the same time he was silent about a Christian church being denied permission to rebuild at that location.

April 2010 – Christian leader Franklin Graham is disinvited from the Pentagon's National Day of Prayer Event because of complaints from the Muslim community.

April 2010 – The Obama administration requires rewriting of government documents and a change in administration vocabulary to remove terms that are deemed offensive to Muslims, including jihad, jihadists, terrorists, radical Islamic, etc.

May 2009 – While Obama does not host any National Day of Prayer event at the White House, he does host White House Iftar dinners in honor of Ramadan.

2010 – While every White House traditionally issues hundreds of official proclamations and statements on numerous occasions, this White House avoids traditional Biblical holidays and events but regularly recognizes major Muslim holidays, as evidenced by its 2010 statements on Ramadan, Eid-ul-Fitr, Hajj, and Eid-ul-Adha.

Many of these actions are literally unprecedented – this is the first time they have happened in four centuries of American history. The hostility of President Obama toward Biblical faith and values is without equal from any previous American president. End of article.

In conclusion

Why are so many comments and references presented above regarding antithesis and attacks on Christians and others who worship God? It reinforces the idea that those being attacked and persecuted for their beliefs need strength to endure and to 'hold fast' to their religious beliefs and their honor to Jesus and God. It's the Spirit of Strength God offers to the entire world to hold fast and endure. The attacks are now great - and will become even greater in the future. (Revelation 2: 25, "But that which ye have already hold fast till I come.")

With the information above, let's now review two important verses presented earlier in this chapter. From Chapter 17, these are: Verse 8: "The beast that thou sawest was, and is not; and shall ascend out of the bottomless pit, and into perdition;..." Verse 11: "And the beast that was, and is not, even he is the eighth, and is of the seven, and goeth into perdition."

Is it possible that the meaning of these two verses could be interpreted as: 'He was of that faith; he left that faith (is not); he returned to that faith and goeth into perdition? Is his strength, and the strength of his followers growing stronger each day in our current-day world? How much strength will Christians and Jews need to withstand the coming tribulation? God has given us that Spirit. Perhaps that strength is encouraged in Chapter 2, Verse 7: "To him that overcometh will I give to eat of the tree of life, which is in the midst of the paradise of God."

This 'tree of life' is identified in Chapter 22, beginning in Verse 2, "In the midst of the street of it, and on either side of the river, was there the tree of life, which bare twelve manner of fruits, and yielded her fruit every month; and the leaves of the tree were for the healing of the nations. 3, And there shall be no more curse; but the throne of God and of the Lamb shall be in it; and his servants shall serve him: 4, and they shall see his face; and his name shall be in their foreheads."

Considering one of those Spirits of God, Wisdom and the resulting responsibility therefrom, should we not use that wisdom to observe and interpret events surrounding us that support the purposes of that other woman - that harlot. God has given us that wisdom for that purpose. Should we ignore to use it; or should we consider all those events happening around us; events that seem uneventful and unimportant? Or should we question events that are surely associated with the growth and influence of that other 'woman?'

How much respect, awe, and support are we giving the Islamic religion today? Remember John's words in 17:6, "And when I saw her, I wondered with great admiration." Is that support not growing rapidly through words, suggestions, and policies of our government, demanded by the president. Are his influences not giving that religion more power and influence, or as the letter to Thyatira suggests; we 'sufferest' that woman Jezebel. In this case, sufferest does not necessarily mean we suffer from; it means we bring pain upon ourselves by our acceptance of and complicity with that woman. The story in Revelation gives us information and warning to prepare for that pain.

Conclusion

The major part of this book has been a condensed review of the Bible's Book of Revelation. Although I have tried to keep it as simple as possible, I'm sure some confusion has been created with all the references and cross-referencing to tie the story together. This was necessary for those sceptics who either don't believe the words in the Bible or who totally despise the mention of God, Christianity or anything associated with God and His promise of salvation.

My aim in this section is to make that story concise, include the implications, and offer a possible necessary preparatory action; since there is now in our great nation, and the entire world, a war on Christianity. That vicious attack is largely allowed by, 'caused' by; and possibly even encouraged by Barack Hussein Obama and his administration. Their actions, deeds, and words do not present the highest level of confidence citizens must have to feel safe within our own country. To what and to whom do they pledge their deepest and most sincere allegiance? It would be wise for all to consider the quote presented at the beginning of this book.

So, I will first summarize the story presented in Revelation intended to warn us of these coming events, and to consider how to prepare for the time of horror and despair that's sure to follow. That time is known as the time of tribulation. It's there; it's in the Bible. Those who refuse to believe and prepare will suffer at their own shallowness, and from that guidance from their god, Satan; even if they have no god.

The Story

The story begins with the seven letters to the seven churches in Asia. Setting the stage before those letters, Christ confirmed who He was and told John to believe him, and not be fooled by others who would claim to be Him. Then he gave those visions of things to come and told John to write the letters.

It seems the letters were only to those seven churches, but coded in the letters were words that meant the letters were aimed at all churches for all times. In effect, the letters were the table of contents for things to come later described in Revelation. In fact, many of those things presented in the letters happened after the time of those churches; they could have in no way understood those events which were to occur seven hundred years later.

Basically, those letters gave only a few important admonitions. The first, and probably the most important, was for those who believed the Word of God to hold fast to those beliefs, because there would be many great deceivers who would try to change them from God. Another caution was to avoid accepting the acts permitted by the Nicolataines; in this case homosexuality and other acts of sexual fornication. But, it seems the greatest admonition offered in those letters was to beware of those who say they are Jews, but are not.

In the case of false Jews he further refined that instruction by introducing the woman, Jezebel, with a description of acts that represent Islam. This included eating things sacrificed to idols and committing fornication. Then he added that He would cast her into that bed of those who commit fornication, and together they would suffer great tribulation. Then He said something very unusual, "And

I will kill her children with death; and all the churches will know that I am he which searcheth the reins and hearts: and I will give unto every one of you according to your works."

Later, in Chapter 17, he explained how that would happen. The two heads of Islam would kill one another, because that was His will. But, before this happened, he announced it would happen earlier when he described the rider of the red horse. He said the rider of the red horse would go forth with a great sword to take peace from the earth and 'to kill one another.' But, there was only one rider. Today, throughout the whole world, that rider still yields his great sword of horror, in service to Satan.

And there was another important warning or admonition in those letters. That was to hold fast to his Word, because He would come suddenly without warning to resurrect those souls who maintain their belief. Be ready, for you don't know the hour that will happen.

The next major event, relatively easy to interpret, was the birth of a woman, a code he used for Christianity. This is explained in Chapter 12. Information in this chapter established the base line for interpreting more parts of Revelation. Verse 14 is the key code that unlocks everything. This chapter says how Christ and Christianity was born, and how young Jesus escaped from being killed during the 'Massacre of the Innocents.' Then Christianity barely survived for the next 350 years, coded as 'time, times, and half a time.' At the end of that time Christianity was adopted by Rome, where she was protected from the beast, Satan, for another 350 years; that 'time, times, and half a time' again. What happened then; 700 years after Christ was born?

That event was described in Chapter 13, with the arrival of a new beast. That beast was described as having seven heads, which many interpret as the seven hills of Rome, and suggest the Pope might be the antichrist - which is totally false. Actually, it means the seven

247

continents. Once that beast, the antichrist, arrived; the dragon, Satan, 'gave him his power, and his seat, and great authority.' That new arrival 'opened his mouth in blasphemy against God, to blaspheme his name, and his tabernacle, and them that dwell in heaven.' Then it was given to him the power to make war with the saints, and many will worship him. Clearly, the one who occupied this antichrist role was none other than Muhammad; 700 years after Christ was born.

After Muhammad's death was described in Verse 10, "He that killeth with the sword must be killed with the sword," then John continues the story with the rise of the Second Beast, also known as the False Prophet. This beast had two horns of a lamb, which made him appear as a man of peace. He deceived many people through his words of peace and convinced many to follow the words of the first beast, that antichirst, Muhammad. This is the one most people believe created the 'mark of the beast.' However, the words do not say he created or demanded that mark. The words say, "He causeth all...to receive that mark. In other words, his words, actions, and inactions allowed that horror to happen. Remember, he is just a man of peace. My interpretation of that mark is explained earlier in this book.

As explained earlier, he didn't make that image to the beast; he caused it to happen, as in a new caliphate in the Middle East. And, he didn't create that mark of the beast in the right hand or in the forehead; instead his actions, words, and inactions caused it to happen. A mark in the forehead simply means one has accepted the words of the beast, and follows him; with a gun in his right hand. No one will have a mark stamped on or in their bodies.

Then John explained the appearance of a little book. An angel invited him to eat the little book; describing when he ate it, it would be as sweet as honey in his mouth; but it would be bitter in his belly. John ate the little book and sure enough, it was as the angel had described. In other words the contents of the book sounded great, but the results of accepting the book was sorrow. Considering all the other codes and descriptions in Revelation, that little book can be no other than what the Muslim's call their Holy Book, their Koran. This story fits with all the other descriptions of Islam in Revelation.

The story builds into a climax of great battles. It's not clear which battles will happen first, but certainly there will be conventional warfare as well as some nuclear activity. Conventional battles are described as locusts and scorpions attacking men, and the crossing of the rivers. Nuclear activity is described as hail falling from the sky mixed with blood. At the end of the battles, the words invite the birds of the sky to come and feast on the flesh of the bodies of those scattered across the hills who had worshiped the beast.

Along within the story are the descriptions of two clear and distinct resurrections. The first resurrection is for those who refused to accept the mark of the beast and were killed for that refusal. It was the great testament of their devotion to God and to his Word. Many of God's martyrs are already being slaughtered in the Middle East, even today for their firm stand with God. Perhaps that's a sign that we are already far along within the story of Revelation. Perhaps we're getting closer to the end without even realizing it. And, there's another possible clue that we are progressing rapidly toward that great battle; before waiting a thousand years for the next one.

That other clue pertains to the current Nuclear agreement with Iran. The time of the agreement is not clear, but it seems to be about seven years; but the participants are clear. Seven, including Iran, will be participants; signatories. Then, consider a verse in Daniel that says midway of that agreement, that beast will void the agreement, and we will enter into a period of tribulation. The signal for that tribulation will be when residents of Jerusalem will have to 'head for the hills' to save themselves. That's described as the 'abomination of desolation.' That's when the beast will enter the holy temple, creating that abomination.

According to the Book, God's forces will win that great battle, and there will be peace on earth for a thousand years. That time is referred to as the Millennium. After that time, Satan will arise from the bottomless pit of fire and brimstone and will go forth to create another war. This time he will be totally defeated. God wins; then adds the exclamation mark.

Now, at this point many believe the earth will come to an end because of the statement of a 'new heaven and a new earth.' However, that doesn't seem to be the case, since there are two verses in the last two chapters that say: "And the nations of them which are saved shall walk in the light of it: and the kings of the earth do bring their glory and honor into it." This is in reference to the new city. Then another, referring to the tree of life in the center of it, "In the midst of the street of it, and on either side of the river, was there the tree of life, which bare twelve manner of fruits, and yielded her fruit every month: and the leaves of the tree were for the healing of the nations."

Certainly, this suggests life will continue on earth even after the Millennium. It says nations will still exist, and if there are nations then there must be people and kings to lead those people.

Then the second resurrection is described earlier in Chapter 20, "But the rest of the dead lived not again until the thousand years were finished." These were judged from the book of life, from which all were judged at that time.

And, at the end of the story God gives hope and a warning. These verses will be cited for clarity from Chapter 22:

Verse 10: "And he saith unto me, Seal not the sayings of the prophecy of this book: for the time is at hand." (He allows everyone to read and understand.)

Verse 11: "He that is unjust, let him be unjust still: and he which is filthy, let him be filthy still: and he that is righteous, let him be righteous still: and he that is holy, let him be holy still.

Verse 12: "And, behold, I come quickly; and my reward is with me, to give every man according as his work shall be."

Verse 13: "I am Alpha and Omega, the beginning and the end, the first and the last."

Warning and Signals

Okay, now that Christ has warned us through John's writings to observe, to be aware, and to do something; what should those things be? He gave several clues throughout, with warnings to be prepared, pay attention, and don't wait. And, putting the whole story into perspective, there are clearly some things he says we must do.

The first signal and suggestion came from the purpose of the black horse, presented by the beast with the face of a man. This wasn't an obvious metaphor like those beasts who presented the other three horses; this was a man, which obviously suggested mankind things. When we think of man and mankind; from the lessons of history we must consider those many times of tribulation: famine, thirst and starvation. The most direct clue was when a voice from the four beasts said, "A measure of wheat for a penny, and three measures of barley for a penny; and see thou hurt not the oil and the wine." So, since the purpose for Revelation; what has he revealed?

Several more clues were very conspicuous throughout the book. The mention of hunger and thirst appeared many times. Added to that was the admonition to 'hurt not the grass and the trees.' What could this mean, putting all these admonitions and warning together? It means that during the time of tribulation there will be a severe shortage or absence of food during that great time. Understanding this is to understand the purpose for the Book of Revelation; it's to warn us to prepare for difficult and harsh times. But, what should we do?

At that time, and it has been calculated to begin three and a half years after that covenant has been signed, already signed, harsh conditions will begin; if not before. Anyone unaware should now be aware; you are reading this alert. And to begin this preparation, following the examples set by those called 'preppers' is the best route.

Serious preppers are prepared with water sources, extra food or knowledge of edible wild plants, alternative food sources, a method of heat, and protection from scavengers who would do you harm to capture your survival assets. "Hurt not the grass and the trees" likely means many of our forests will be destroyed by the millions of people on earth burning those trees for heat and for cooking - primitive survival.

And, please, please, don't be influenced by Obama and his leftist followers: you must own a weapon. You won't be able to call 911 for help. And - Obama and his leftist group who try to keep you from owning a defensive weapon will not really care what happens to you. They will slink into the darkness, fade into the sunset, and swear they were real patriots. Believe them now as you would then.

If every true American owns a weapon, and that fact is announced to Satan's world, we likely would never have to fire a single shot to defend ourselves. They would know our resolve not to be defeated by Satan. Our time of tribulation would be minimized. And, when you buy a weapon, make sure you can buy ammunition for that weapon at the same time; or you might not find ammunition at a later date. That will be the first item to be limited or restricted if and when the ban is considered, since many family guns passed down through generations are not registered or accountable through the purchase process. Controlling availability of ammunition is the only way to control use of these old weapons; and it will happen.

Islamaphobe or Islamaknowbe

You have already read that document titled: The Explanatory Memorandum on The General Strategic Goal For the Group in North America. It's the document that encouraged all Muslim organizations and activities to become part of that strategic goal. The goal announced in that document is to destroy North America by consuming it with a process called Settlement. The Council on American-Islamic Relations (CAIR) was one of many organizations listed as one of its members.

The main goal of CAIR is to defend that Islamic Strategic Goal by labeling anyone who criticizes or says anything negative about Islam or Muslims as an Islamaphobe or as Islamaphobic. If you will watch carefully, when you see these words used, ordinarily it's that organization CAIR promoting it. As a result, many people are more and more reluctant to say anything about Islam; they will be tagged with that label. It's now synonymous with 'Racist.'

If they don't like what someone says, the instant response is to label them an Islamaphobe or a Racist. They use those words because there's no defense against them. Therefore, we need a new defense to combat CAIR and other groups who use those terms to disarm someone who's fighting for our country and our heritage; and to preserve our culture. We need something to instantly disarm that attack. And, there is one.

What could be that new defense? I suggest we promote ourselves as 'Islamaknowbic.' or an 'Islamaknowbe.' This would slap back in their faces that we 'know' what your Islam is and we 'know' who you are: the Mother of Harlots. And this word would also profess that we 'know' where you come from. You are the rider of the 'red horse'

(Revelation 6:4) that goes forth to kill one another and take peace from the earth. And we can even add another recognition that we 'know:'

You are that same rider of the scarlet beast full of names of blasphemy against God (17:3) who is identified as 'Mystery, Babylon the Great, the Mother of Harlots and Abominations of the Earth:' drunken with the blood of the saints, and with the blood of the martyrs of Jesus. (17:5-6.)

Islam has 'taken peace from the earth' and Her Harlots are the terrorists who are committing murders, abominations and atrocities throughout the world. And they are, as the rider of the red horse, killing one another; including Mother Islam. If they have been touched by Satan, he will totally control them when the time is ripe.

Yes, we know who you are: we are now Islamaknowbic. I encourage everyone to read that detailed Memorandum. It's clearly available. Then, you will 'know' all about who they are and their plans to destroy us. What reply could they have to an 'Islamaknowbe?' They will know that we know; and we understand. It would turn the concept around; they would have no defense against it if we let them know how much we know about them in only one word: Islamaknowbe. And add, "You will not destroy us who know."

The Apocalypse is not something in the future; it's begun.

God Bless America

About The Author

Will Clark's author experiences began by writing inspection and evaluation reports in the U.S. Air Force. He is a retired Air Force officer and a Vietnam veteran, serving in Saigon from 1966 to 1967. His other overseas assignments include Misawa, Japan and Ankara, Turkey; where he visited the ancient sites of the Seven Churches.

In 1995, as a 'Friends of Education' study skills project, he authored a book, *How to Learn*, to encourage students to improve their grades in DeSoto County, Mississippi. Education supporters printed and distributed four thousand copies. The following school year he wrote a weekly education column for a local newspaper, *The DeSoto County Tribune*. He also taught an adult GED class. His book, *How to Learn*, has been updated and is now available everywhere.

His next published book was *School Bells and Broken Tales*, a parody of nursery rhyme characters, also a motivation and education book for children. Other books include *Shades of Retribution,* a historical novel, and *Simply Success*, a motivation guide for students and employees.

His action novel, The Atlantis Crystal, is the first of a trilogy based on Atlantis and crystals. The other two books are: *She Waits in Atlantis*, and *Return to Atlantis*. This trilogy is based on his travels while assigned to Turkey, site of the ancient city of Troy. His latest political thriller is: *America 20XX: The New World Order.*

The past five years he has devoted his full time to the study, research, and writing of an analysis of the Book of Revelation and the danger of Satan, that beast that guides Islam.

Things We Must Never Forget
Until We Know All the Answers

Benghazi

Why were four Americans killed?
Where was Hillary Clinton while it was happening?
Where was Barack Obama while it was happening?
Why did they lie and blame the event on a video?
Why were rescuers on 'stand by' told to 'stand down?'

Fast and Furious

Who authorized the operation?
Why did the operation continue after weapons were lost?
Why did the procedure have no procedure?
Why weren't tracking devices used?

The IRS Scandal

What was the highest level involved?
Who initiated it?
Why hasn't anyone been fired or reprimanded?
What dangers could be unleashed by this organization?

Greatest Quotes
of Our Time

Michelle Obama
February 18, 2008
"For the first time in my adult life I am proud of my country."
(Age 44)

Barack Obama
March 9, 2008
"We are no longer a Christian nation - at least not just."

September 25, 2012
Remarks to the UN General Assembly
"The future must not belong to those who slander Islam."

Nancy Pelosi
March 9, 2010
"We have to pass the bill so that you can find out what is in it."

Hillary Clinton
January 23, 2013
"What difference, at this point, does it make?"

December 3, 2014
"...showing respect even for one's enemies, trying to understand
and insofar as psychologically possible, empathize with their
perspective and point of view."

Other Books by the Author

Novels:
Shades of Retribution
The Atlantis Crystal
She Waits in Atlantis
Return to Atlantis
America 20XX: The New World Order
666: Mark of the Beast
Death Drones: 2025

Children's Books:
Forest Trails and Fairy Tales
Wishing Wells and Broken Tales
Student Study Skills
American Heroes: Students Who Learn

Non-Fiction:
Simply Success
The Education Jungle
How to Learn
The Day America Died
Obama's Ring: The Seat of Satan
Managing Without Conflict
The Peer Pressure Monster
Denied 3 Times
The War on Christians
Who is the Antichrist
Islamic Two-Headed Beast
Islam Attacks the Whore
The Second Beast
Secrets of the Seven Churches
Two Woman of the Apocalypse
Islam's Bloodthirsty Sword

www.ingramcontent.com/pod-product-compliance
Lightning Source LLC
Chambersburg PA
CBHW071335280526
45787CB00001B/100

* 9 7 8 1 5 2 2 7 5 3 5 5 1 *